CW01619799

One Breath

One Step

One Second

At A Time

Stuart Humber

3P
2

First published in 2025 in the UK

3P2, Tailby House,
Bath Road, Kettering
NN16 8NL

A catalogue number for this book is available from the British Library

ISBN: 978-1-913740-76-4

Cover design: James Mossop

Contents:

Introduction

With the sombre tones of B. B. King dominating my air space, and the hood of my gym jacket draped over my head blocking out any peripheral vision so as to isolate myself from any distractions from the outside world, I started wavering about the thought of actually writing a second book. My first book, 'Don't Fail at Failure', being the massive number one best-selling hit in my hometown of Lutterworth during the month of June 2021, I was feeling a bit anxious to start again. 'Don't Fail at Failure' was mainly about my coming of age and lifting myself back up time after time from a life full of continual falls, addictions, kicks and misfortunes. With the concluding fairy tale ending of me finishing the 380-mile virtual 6633 Arctic Ultra in such an amazing and dramatic fashion.

Perched on the end of my sofa with a blank screen in front of me some three years after writing the first part of this story, I started contemplating. Do I actually have a second part to the story? Do I even want or need to throw some words together again? And, simply, do I have time to finish what I'm about to start? On the one hand I thoroughly enjoyed writing the first book, as I fell head over heels into the whole experience. From the initial thought-provoking dream I had when I excitedly woke up at 3am with the concept of writing a book, to receiving the delivery of the finished product six months later. The counselling, release and self-awareness I gained from hours upon hours of solitude whilst sharing myself and my thoughts with every tap of the keyboard was addictively seductive.

On the other hand, though, the thought of starting another project felt overwhelming, especially as I didn't feel the drive this time, or even the necessity to share. Also, reading my first book again, in the hope it would inspire me to strike the keys with conviction once more, I was actually shocked at my original achievement. I was so proud of what I had managed to create, and felt that I didn't want to dilute the quality of the first book by writing a follow-up and creating something that felt forced. By no means would my first book warrant any literal accolades or be compared with any of the deep-thinking psychologists of our world, but I was in awe of my own accomplishment. A large percentage of my thoughts were heading towards, 'quit whilst you're ahead'.

Six months of Shall I's, or Shan't I's, and I came to the conclusion, that will be obvious to you now because you are starting to read it, that I should.

The reasons being: Firstly, nothing had changed from the initial reason of wanting to put pen to paper a few years ago in order to leave something to future generations of my family, giving them a true understanding of who I was, and basically giving me a little bit of immortality. Also, a helpful guide for them to hopefully progress through life with a little less pain and uncertainty in this difficult and rapidly-changing world. And as always, the bonus would be if anyone else stumbled across my story and connected with it; that would make the whole process even more worthwhile.

Secondly, the story wasn't finished as I hadn't said everything I wanted to say, and I still had to make it to, be successful in, and write about my journey to the Canadian Arctic. The race that still haunts me, 'The

6633 Arctic Ultra'. The toughest, coldest and windiest self-sufficient footrace on the planet. It still needed ticking off. The concluding part of this journey still had to be completed, along with the education, growth and adaptation required to get me to the start line and to achieve one of my dreams by crossing the finishing line. This all needs to be logged, shared and passed on, all the lessons and stories, along with all the ups and downs.

We also still needed to talk about the two doors you face every day and my five pillars of health, which can ultimately give you the best chance at grabbing life by the horns. We need to discuss how dealing with every single moment of life by taking it a breath, a step and a second at a time is the only way to do it. We haven't touched on resilience, standing back up after falling, being stoic in the face of misfortune, or understanding that life is an infinite game, not a finite game. It's not something that can be won, but something that can only be taken part in. Being a daydreamer, dancing in the rain, keeping your shit to yourself and not fearing the reaper, all need to be written about, read, and then time taken to understand. These and other life lessons that I've gathered in my first half a century on this rock are things I want to pass on to my kids, my kids' kids, and anyone else who has nothing better to do on a Sunday afternoon than read another number one bestseller from this infamous author, ultra athlete, and best Health Coach in the world.....One can always dream.

And lastly; why the hell not? What else am I going to do to keep my head straight? Who else am I supposed to talk to about all this shit? I've already heard it all. It's time to awaken those creative juices, become my own counsellor and share the rest of this journey that will hopefully take me to the finish of something spectacular.

Let's get emotional one more time....

Chapter 1

What's behind door number two?

Not failing at failure has become so ingrained into the Humber household that I'm beginning to feel it has become a little overused, a little insignificant, even annoying, especially when my daughters roll their eyes whenever I bring it up.

Finishing the virtual version of the 6633 Arctic Ultra was unquestionably the hardest physical exploit I have ever undertaken. The whole journey through 12 months of training, preparation, practising and evolving, and a lifetime of knocks, kicks, falls, weaknesses, and incompetence within relationships, in finances, in health, basically in life, were all vitally important and necessary in the success of this challenge. Whilst writing my first book 'Don't Fail at Failure', (I'll keep plugging it), I discovered how important it is to have the right people in my life. I reevaluated time, and how spending it wisely with the right people was a priority, especially spending quality time with myself, because making me the best version of myself would benefit everyone else around me as a consequence. I became acquainted with Melvin, my mischievous monkey, who sits on my shoulder constantly whispering in my ear, willing me to eat crap, drink alcohol, skip classes, spend money, stay up late and generally be an idiot. But, once an understanding and communication pathway had been established with this little pain in the arse, he can be a very powerful and a stony-eyed adversary when needed. I also painfully discovered the meaning of the phrase 'Fail to prepare, prepare to fail', putting not just my life but a friend's life in danger whilst hiking across England on the Coast to Coast. I developed a passion for passion, along with the need for a journey and the value in taking risks. I woke up to the realisation that instant gratification is a pandemic, a pandemic that is suffocating the first world, creating a generation full of depression, anxiety and stress. All of this led to me morphing from an overweight, unhappy, unsympathetic and selfish individual to a healthier, fitter, empathetic and driven health club owner with a wife now free from disability and two amazing daughters who look up to me as a father and not a dictator.

The first book was a hell of a journey, but as mentioned, there was still a long way to go. I had more to learn and more to teach. Understanding we are never the finished product, as we pass through the days and weeks trying to sculpt a life, by ticking boxes, stepping over boulders, and battling through walls, was another important lesson I wanted to pass on. We feel these walls and barriers are deliberately placed in front of us to piss us off and destroy our happiness, by whatever we imagine is in the sky. The first thing we always do when problems mount up, and we are at the end of our rope is look to the clouds and ask the question, why me? Box after box and obstacle after obstacle seem to be thrown in our way, hindering our progress, punishing us, and slowing us down. It's not until we've travelled further down the road and look back that we realise that these challenging times were necessary for us to learn new skills, develop new coping strategies and build new strengths, enabling us to progress to the next level. We will only have the resolve to break through the next wall when we've grown from the last one.

When a wall, a barrier, an obstacle, or basically anything so enormous, so intimidating and so overwhelming is placed in front of you; something so terrifying that it halts any further progress in any direction until it's overthrown; in fact, something so huge that it casts a shadow over anything else of any significance in your life, you'll have to become a different person to get through it. You have to become a new version of yourself, a version that has taken some hits, felt the growth needed, stood back up, and then developed the resilience to move forward again. A person that has had to bleed, sweat, cry, grow and evolve into a new entity that will eventually understand how to break the barrier down or even climb over it to achieve something that used to be so unimaginable. By doing this, by becoming the butterfly, by mutating into a totally different creature in order to achieve your objective, you must, and you will, wake up a part of your soul, a part of your spirit, that cannot go back to sleep. Every time you overcome adversity, every time you find the strength to stand back up, you open up more life, more options and more of the true you, which slowly, but surely wakes up a sleeping giant.

This transition, this metamorphosis, this journey can create a spark that ignites a flame, a flame that, much like the Olympic torch, cannot go out until the game is over. It cannot be blown out or extinguished and it cannot be suffocated by darkness. This flame illuminates a new doorway that could provide an alternative way of life, a different way of seeing the world, that is, if you choose to open it. Let's call this new doorway, door number two. This newly-visible doorway now gives you options. Option one; is door number one, the door that once you step through it, you find yourself on the journey which has been subliminally educated to you from the very first day you inhaled oxygen, guiding you through every single decision you have ever made that has led to you reading this book, in your house, that has been funded by your chosen career and enabling you to share your life with all the people you have chosen to be part of it. Basically, the semi-predictable future that is comfortably laid out in front of you. But now you also have option two, also known as door number two, a door that could be exciting and unpredictable, a door that could give you freedom, but could equally get you into a world of trouble.

Whilst writing my first book, I woke up to the notion that my journey was somewhat within my control, and not the inevitable outcome of the A to Z mundanity of the world we have subconsciously created to follow. Every morning as our eyes open, we have a choice, a choice to walk through one of these two doors. Door number one is the door that follows the safe journey. This is the journey that has rules, regulations, do's and don'ts, barriers, hazard tape, restrictions, guidelines, security and a clear, well-presented and illustrated service manual. This will then take you through the days, weeks, months and years, ultimately a lifetime, on a comfortable soft cushion wrapped in cotton wool. Behind this door is the 2.4 children, the loyal labrador, the detached house on a lovely housing estate with a BMW parked in front, a comfortable pension built on the back of large corporations, two holidays a year, one in the sun and one in the snow, and a life written by Walt Elias Disney himself. Sounds perfect, right? Yes, it definitely does, and there is absolutely nothing wrong with that door. It's safe, secure, loving, and reliable, and who doesn't want to feel part of a fairy tale? To me though, it has always felt too regimented, too dictated and too expected. It's always made me feel like I'm part of an ant colony; walk in line, do as you're told, think about the big picture, do your bit for the empire and you will be rewarded with a small piece of the pie if you make it to the end of the fight. I never really felt alive or a true part of my own story whilst trying to disneyfy my life, and I always knew that someone else was getting more of my pie than me.

I'm sorry Walt, but I never did believe in fairy tales, and I really can't stand housing estates, although I do love labradors as well as all the other shapes and sizes of woofers. That is, apart from those little creatures that seem to grow out of handbags. Those little gremlins have had my fingers on numerous occasions! I needed another option. I needed an option away from the social norm, away from the straight lines and away from this bloody housing estate I live in. Just because my body resides in this suburb doesn't mean my mind has to. Then it happened. Something woke up during those six and a half days and 383 miles of the virtual 6633 Arctic Ultra. The spark, the flame and that magical door number two, which, trust me, is by far more magical than anything Mr Disney had ever promised lurking behind door number one.

Door number two is the door that takes you on a journey full of surprise, ups and downs, torture and triumph, tears and laughter, love and hate, late nights and early mornings, fortunes and depressions. A life that creates opportunity, growth, wisdom, experience, and an awakening of your true potential. It opens your eyes to the world around you, the real beauty of nature and how disturbingly horrendous it can be. It brings limitless possibilities, adventures and freedom, a life full of risk, adrenaline, emotions and gambles, but a life that, I believe, would give me, and you, a great satisfaction in our final days. It's not a life that everyone could handle, and once again, there is absolutely nothing wrong with that. In fact, the world wouldn't have progressed in the way it has if we all lived like we'd walked through the second doorway, and there is a massive part of me that would love to be content with door number one. After all, let's face it, Disney is very good at creating a 'Happily forever after'.

The question is now over to you, which door will you open today now you know they both exist? The decision sounds easy, right? At the end of the day, who wants a life where the pages are already written; who wants a life where you can't breathe, where you can't be yourself and where you are unable to spread your wings? Staring at the two doors each morning whilst still trying to focus through glazed eyes, knowing a decision will inevitably be made either consciously or subconsciously, and knowing that, depending on this decision, you will either have a day full of possibilities, life, growth and progression, or a day full of the A to Z that has been described and drilled into you throughout your earliest years. Ask yourself, do you really want another day with the same outcome as yesterday and the day before and the day before that; do you really want another day of just existing? Understanding what's on offer behind each door, the answer should be easy, I would hope. The answer is, of course, you would choose the life of adventure, opportunity and possibility, rather than the mundanity.

There is a catch however, because as I have vaguely mentioned before, this isn't an 'open and shut case' because once door number two has been opened and you've stepped through it, it can't be closed again, and all the protection, all the cushioning and all the guidelines have gone. You're on your own. Your life is now in your own hands. It can be very scary and actually very isolating. In my experience, most people find it hard to relate to other people that live behind door number two. You'll find you don't fit into the same boxes, you don't watch soap operas or reality TV shows, you don't care what player got sold to what team for what amount of ridiculous money. You don't finger point, categorise people or bow-down to the labelling of ists or isms, or sexualities, religions, nationalities, colours, or even if someone decides they want to be known as a different identity. People are just bloody people, and this makes most of society infuriated. The fact that you don't have an opinion or care for most of the world's news will make you unrelatable. You will have absolutely no shit to give when the overly-opinionated try to suck you into a discussion about the comings and goings of the new couple who've moved into number 36, and it pisses them off. It nearly angers them as much when they realise you have no opinion of the political party that is now running the country, never mind your region, and to add to this, you have no intention of voting at next week's general election because you realise that the whole thing is a farce and people are only voting for the party they believe will leave them with the most money in their pockets. They don't really give a shit about the health service, or education, unemployment statistics or the environment. It always has been and always will be just a money vote. Ironically, they don't realise the whole charade is about which party is the cleverest at taking money out of their pocket without them knowing it. It's like taking a vote on whether to be hit by a baseball bat or a cricket bat, hoping you pick the one that will hurt the least. What I am saying is, as you open door two and start feeling this beautiful world for what it is and the unfortunate corruption that tries to control it, you'll think differently than others and become, as I said, isolated. You'll only truly connect with people who see it the same way, the people that have also chosen to live behind door number two, and, unfortunately, they number only a few out of the masses.

If you do decide to partake in the road less travelled, the question is, what are you going to do with it? Which direction will you take it? What opportunities will you gamble on? How will you find your true potential? Do you have a limit and what happens when you reach it? How can you possibly know who you are; what sort of father or mother you will be or what kind of friend or colleague you will be, until you've answered some of these questions. More importantly, what comes after you have answered these questions? What will you have learned? How much will you have grown? What adaptations would have been created enabling you to reach your crown and glory? Could finding these answers make you more content, happy, wise, balanced and self-knowing? What benefits could be felt that affect other avenues of your life? Could it make you a better mother, father, wife or husband? Could it make you more successful in your career? Calmer under pressure, more equipped at multitasking, or emotionally controlled when situations go to pot? If you know exactly who you are, at what point you break, what you can push through, and what happens when you go further than you knew possible, then wouldn't that make you far more powerful than you could have ever imagined.

As far as I was concerned my door number two was now gaping wide open and seductively drawing me in during every waking moment, and with the adrenaline still pumping through my veins after finishing 383 miles in 6 and a half days in front of everyone who loves me, along with knowing that the job wasn't actually truly finished yet, I set a training programme that would see me to the start line of the official 6633 Arctic Ultra in February the following year. The training started the day after the virtual finish with another 20 miles in the bag, and continued with this intensity until the end of March. My accumulated mileage in March finished at an incredible 800.2 miles followed by another 500+ miles in April. I was obsessed, it became an addiction, an unhealthy addiction. Everything else around me was beginning to break. My body was hurting, joints were grinding, muscles were knotting, and only connective tissues were holding me together. Work was a second thought; I would go through the motions, but I was never really present. My clients paid hard earned money for my time and they deserved more. All I could think about was how I would be able to get my 20-30 miles in today if I had 8 - 10 hours of coaching, household duties to uphold, energy to give to my loved ones, dogs to walk and sleep to squeeze in. I started resenting clients for booking in more sessions. My relationships obviously started suffering. Talking stopped with my wife and daughters. We never went out, never had fun, and barely ate together. I would pass out half way through the evening meal, get up at 4am every morning to walk or run 10-20 miles before work, and I lost valuable and necessary time with friends. Nothing was heading to a happy place. Once again, my addictive nature found a way of changing a light, healthy obsession into a black hole that would suck energy from everything within its gravitational reach to keep it alive. If I, my family unit, my career and everything I had built, worked towards and established was going to survive, I needed to find balance. If I was going to make it to the arctic and get through the races and challenges I had planned this year without screwing everything else up, I had to adapt.

Truth be told, I felt and knew every single day of 2021 that I was in trouble, but convinced myself that the answer to all my problems was at the edge of a small village called Tuktoyaktuk somewhere along the coast of the Arctic Ocean in the Northern Territories of Canada. Everyone would forgive me for my lack of presence if I succeeded in making it to the end of the 383-mile road. My business would grow, finances would improve, I'd feel more love and be able to give more love, balance would return, and our future would be secure. There was no alternative. I couldn't see a world without success, without a win, without a victory to give to my family, friends and work colleagues. I needed to persevere for my sake, for their sake; after all, I was doing it all for them!

I know, I know… you are already thinking, what I naively ignored… but let me finish the story.

To get me through the year and to keep me focused, as if I needed any more focus, I revisited a couple of my old haunts and introduced myself to a couple of new ones. 'The Race to the Stones', which is a 100km race in the centre of England along the ridgeway path, one of the oldest pathways in the UK, finishing in the ancient village of Avebury. This is still my best performance in any race. I finished 27th out of over 1,200 participants in a brilliant time of 10 hours 40 ish minutes. The South Downs 100-miler along the South Down Way's beautiful pathway in the south of England, but unfortunately I got pulled out after 16 hours at the 73 mile checkpoint from heat exhaustion when the mercury was hovering around 32 degrees. A first time visit to my favourite-ever race called the Classic Quarter, a very beautiful, very scenic and very undulating race of 44 miles and 10,000ft of vert along the coastal path of Cornwall from Lizard Point, England's southernmost point, to Lands End, the westernmost point of England. Once again, performing well and arriving at the finishing arch in just under 9 hours, and feeling proud that only 23 people of the 350 racers finished more quickly than me. These three main races and a couple of small local ultras filled my summer and autumn, keeping my mind quiet and my diary full. I constantly acknowledged I had a problem but chose to run through it, even being ignorant to the fact that my family's holiday locations were based on the locations of my races. During the four months of the summer I built up 2,500 miles of training and events, and by the time I was cooling down for the arctic race in February 2022, I had accumulated 5,200 miles in 11 months, charging through anything that might get in the way, including eight pairs of Hokas. I'm surprised I didn't have to pay road tax as my car hadn't done that many miles and it probably used less rubber.

At the beginning of this chapter, I explained how exhilarating the new door could be and how it was going to be my saviour, my freedom and my light. It would open my eyes to a new life, taking me down a path full of rose petals, rainbows, love, and inspiration. It definitely opened my eyes, but it wasn't just my eyes it opened. It opened something else that made it impossible for me to feel content with the world around me. It felt like I had taken a drug that made me feel awakened, a drug that made me feel separate from reality and unable or unwilling to be part of it, a drug that now left me with a hole I had no idea how to fill, which is why I tried to shovel mile after mile into it, filling the void with bling and achievements. I was hoping the miles would take away the isolation and return me back to the ignorance of not knowing a door number two even existed. A part of me just wanted to go back to the ant colony. A part of me wished I'd taken the blue pill, If you know what I mean. But as mentioned, once you've stepped through that door there is no going back. A new form of depression, anxiety and dis-satisfaction was waiting for me on the other side of the door. It had been triggered because I didn't yet know how to find fulfilment, happiness, acceptance or contentment with a life that didn't align with a world that, for the most part, didn't know or care about a door number two. I was now living outside the matrix wishing, for the most part, that I could be re-entered. Sometimes ignorance is bliss, but then again, sometimes knowledge is power. I spent most days over the next few months swaying back and forth from feeling honoured that I was now awake and being pissed off because I was now awake. Eventually I came to the conclusion that the world is what it is; it hasn't changed, it was me that had changed. I just needed to adapt my thinking and my energy to sing to the same tune as the world I lived in, but sing it my way. The problem was that I still couldn't even reach a single note, never mind make a tune, not until this task was accomplished. I convinced myself that I just needed to finish what I started and tick this 6633 box that had been haunting me for the last two winters. Once this box had been ticked, I would be able to sing like a canary. When I say two years, it's actually been nine years since this race made me take a very big, long, hard look at myself back in 2013. Before I was able to sing, I needed to show to myself, and everyone connected to me, that the last nine years of me waking up every single day and pushing myself to the limit to be better at everything I could possibly improve in, was worth it. I needed that medal. I needed a conclusion. I had to finish this chapter of my life and show to everyone that I'd cracked it. I needed to show I was better, more in control, stronger and more disciplined.

Once again, I know what you're thinking…

WHAT A LOAD OF BOLLOCKS. I didn't know it at the time, but bollocks. Just another stroke of my ego, that's all I was after. My achievements over the last nine years were shown on the faces, in the hearts, and through the lives of everyone that meant anything to me, and to whom I meant something to. The rewards of my efforts and the changes I'd made were shown to me on a daily basis in so many ways, but I was blinded by these tunnel-visioned glasses. All I could see, all I cared about, was how hard I had worked and how much sacrifice I had made. I had put in more hours, more sweat and more pain than anyone else who stood on the start line in February 2022. I had earned the bloody right to get to the end of it this time. All I could see was Tuk and the Arctic Ocean.

Chapter 2

Hands down.

October 2021 came, along with another email from the event crew of the 6633 Arctic Ultra. This email, similar to the one received exactly a year before, explained that the race as we know it, the race I've been neglecting everyone and everything for, for the past two and half bloody years, could still not go ahead. The email went through the reasons why the Northwest Territories district of Canada still refused to allow outsiders into their region. Basically, they were still fearful that someone would bring Covid to their small communities. I did understand and sympathise, as it's so hard to get and receive medical assistance in such remote places, and people were still very much living on the edge, but fuck!

There was, however, an alternative. Assuming enough participants were willing to have a go, the organiser would set up a route further down the Dempster Highway. This would start at the beginning of the Dempster Highway, up and over the Tombstone National Park, and then continue all the way to the Arctic circle sign 250 miles away. This is where the Yukon district changes to the Northwest Territories. The Yukon at this point had opened its doors and was moving forward from the pandemic, making this a totally feasible option. It was an option that had never been looked at or done before, but doable. This section of the Dempster, in my opinion, is the most stunning part of the 460-mile road which winds its way from just outside Dawson City to Inuvik. This 250-mile section has over 12,000 feet of elevation, meaning it has a substantial amount more than the classic 383 miler I had been training for. The price tag for this event would be a lot cheaper too, because we would be the guinea pigs to see if this would be feasible as an annual event. It took a whole five minutes for me to decide, of which four minutes fifty seconds of this was spent explaining the situation to Teri. So, with my thumbs up to the race, along with another nine similarly unstable athletes, we just had enough interest to make the trip happen.

The rest of the winter came more quickly than expected, and at the end of February it was wheels up from London's Heathrow Airport, and wheels down in Whitehorse, Canada. Accompanying me on the flight were a few other athletes, and you can always tell which of the other passengers on the plane are ultra runners because of their stony, weathered features and their colourful expensive attire, which never matched, and were made more for convenience than for comfort. Once all our luggage had been collected, we hopped into a convoy of black 4x4's which led us to our accommodation along with the crew support. Whitehorse was a lot bigger than I remember from nine years ago. It had more of a commercial feel to it. The energy of a sleepy town I had described to others whilst reminiscing and telling stories about my adventures in 2013, had changed into an active community. Don't get me wrong; for the size of the town, there was only a fraction of the hustle and bustle you would expect from a fully functioning community. It still had its unemployment problem, with a lot of locals living off state-provided incomes. They would wander the streets in the middle of the afternoon with a skin full of the cheapest liquor available and carrying the potent smell of marijuana. The heaviness of the scent could give the innocent bystander the munchies if they stayed out in it for too long.

Every time I go to Canada the Jet lag ruins me for days, as it constantly wakes me up at 2am, and I wasn't alone with this problem. We'd all end up congregating in the reception of the hotel sharing stores and waiting for a coffee machine to be switched on anywhere in the neighbourhood. As the day greeted us on the first morning away from home, we all drifted out of the hotel in small groups in search of subsistence. With another athlete I eventually found my grazing pasture a few streets away where we stopped for a coffee and a pastry treat for breakfast. It was a lovely morning. The sun was casting shadows of the buildings across the street, and as we sat outside the coffee shop enjoying a strong cup of wake-me-up, feeling the sun's slight heat comfortably connect with the little bit of skin showing, a local man scuffled past. He was maybe in his late 30's and was accompanied by his collie-cross pet dog. They both sat on a bench a couple of metres away from us with no expression on either of their faces, no acknowledgement of the environment they were in or the people around them. Both sitting stony faced staring into the abyss in front of them, he was red eyed and the dog with a slightly relaxed tongue hanging from its mouth. Obviously and undeniably both stoned. As the sun progressed slightly higher into the sky, the shadow of the building opposite drifted down the dastardly duo's torsos exposing their eyes to the glare of the morning's rays. With no emotion the guy slipped his right hand into his inside left jacket pocket, pulled out a pair of sunglasses with green rims and placed them in position, bridging his nose. Then, with his left hand, he went into his inside right jacket pocket and pulled out another pair of sunglasses with orange rims and placed them across the nose of his dog. This all happened without either of them changing their expressions from the emptiness in front of them. Totally mind-blown, the two of us let loose with an uncontrollable burst of laughter, shaking our heads in disbelief. We commented on the man's dog saying how much we loved its companionship and acceptance. He replied without moving a muscle, apart from his chubby tanned cheeks, and once again, without showing emotion, “he helps me get the chick’s, best wing man I’ve ever had”. This totally did me in; I was in hysterics, I was gone, and I lived off that image for days. One of the coolest things I’ve ever seen.

Anyway, onto the important stuff. We spent seventy-two hours in Whitehorse, and it flew by as everyone disappeared into sled-building, food-prepping, kit trials and checks, shopping, meetings and briefings, and maybe the odd pint. I always love a good race briefing. The best ones always seem to get the right balance of just terrifying you enough, so you question your sanity whilst covering enough to make you believe you're safe-ish and capable of ‘just’ finishing. The pre-race shopping spree also gives me a little chuckle, as athletes discover, during dinner table chit-chat, that another racer might have a little tool or piece of clothing or idea that they hadn’t thought of which might give them the edge. So, like a herd of wildebeest charging away from their predators, they descend on the local outlets with just as much fear in their eyes as the wildebeest would have. They were terrified of the thought that they could be the one that fails getting to the end of the race because they had missed out on that vitally important piece of equipment that they knew they wouldn't need and would further weigh their sled down.

All boxes ticked. I found myself lying on my hotel bed the night before departure at 3am crying as I watched a cheap rom-com while doing an outstanding impersonation of Bridget Jones. I was lying there feeling sorry for myself and slightly angry about the direction my life must have taken that led to me being here, on my own, and about to embark on another stupid, unnecessary, ridiculously hard challenge in minus 30 degrees Celsius thousands of miles away from my family. The only thing I had left to eat to comfort my melancholy was some peanut butter which I skilfully spread onto the remaining animal crackers with the end of my toothbrush. Everything else had been packed into my sled and drop bags before giving them to the event organisers for transport to the start line some 500 miles north, just outside Dawson City. Anyone looking in would have seriously questioned how this blubbering mess, sucking peanut butter off of a toothbrush, could even contemplate trying to survive on his own for five days in such an unforgiving environment. It's a good job the crew didn't see me, or I would have been instantly pulled from the race.

Moments later, in what seemed like a blink of an eye, I snapped out of my daze covered in crumbs, melted chocolate and peanut butter, as the alarm alerted me it was 6am. A few seconds later, realising where I was and what was expected of me, I ventured down for a quick bite to eat and a strong cup of tar before finding my place in one of the five big ass American four wheel drives to head in hot pursuit of the sleds and drop bags which had left earlier for Dawson.

We hit our destination just after the sun set that day; the regularly-used Downtown Hotel in Dawson City, to have one more night in a comfortable bed. The Downtown Hotel is famous for being the only place in the world to sell a cocktail called 'A Sourtoe cocktail'. This cocktail, and I say this with my hand on heart, I swear, has a detached frost-bitten human toe in it. Unfortunately, the bar was presently closed because of Covid restrictions, so we all missed out. I didn't mind too much because I had the privilege of experiencing this extraordinary drink on my first visit a few years ago. You'll need to check out the first chapter of my previous book 'Don't Fail at Failure' to find out how that went….I hope you appreciated the little sales pitch I managed to get in there.

Morning arrived before I was willing to accept it, but time wasn't going to hang around for me to grow a pair. So, an hour or so later, I was dressed for success with a belly full of fried potatoes, eggs and bacon, and heading towards the mouth of the Dempster Highway. This is where a gun would be fired alerting us to begin putting one foot in front of the other continuously for 250 miles.

With a startling bang we set off with dreams in our heads, ambition in our hearts, and enough caffeine in our legs to fuel an army. I started with such vigour and drive that within a few miles I was clearly out in front and marching through the most beautiful start of a race I have ever experienced. Heavily snow-ladened trees were on both sides of the slightly inclining but rolling road, which was visible for miles. A few hundred metres behind was Rio, who was from Canada, and then Vlad from Romania. I still don't know why, but Vlad clearly showed, on a daily basis, that we were not going to be friends. It was his fourth visit to the race and still came looking for his first finish. I had beaten him by nearly a day on the virtual race the previous year, so maybe he was trying to intimidate me. O well, poor fella.

The first checkpoint to Tombstone Campground was 44 miles up the road and actually felt pretty comfortable. Rio caught up with me after a few miles and we continued to yoyo past each other all the way to that first checkpoint. I passed him on the uphills and he returned the favour on the downs. Occasionally we would walk side by side to share a few stories. We both started to feel quite comfortable in each other's presence, chatting away whilst creating a further lead on everyone else. Rio was a young lad, barely old enough to take part in the race. He lived fairly locally and had a plan to tour the world over the next eighteen months, including a visit to England where we later caught up with each other while he squatted at my home for a few days.

There was a point about thirty miles into the first section where I had managed to pull away from Rio by a mile or so when something unforgettable happened. I was comfortably gliding along in my own world, listening to absolutely nothing. I do love nothing; it's totally refreshing, very simple and emotionally powerful to feel that connection to nothing, pure nothingness. We all need to experience nothing every now and again. It's so fulfilling and absorbing. I could have stayed in the moment for hours, if not, days, but just as I was drifting peacefully away something touched my hand. I looked down and couldn't see anything, so guessing it must have been part of my deep-thinking imagination. I shrugged my shoulders and carried on. A moment later I got another nudge, a little firmer this time. That was definitely real. Sharply looking down to my right and jumping out of my skin whilst letting out a gasping cry of 'a wolf', a fucking wolf, I'm dead, this is it, I'm done for. A second later, as my rational hormones kicked back in, I realised It wasn't a wolf but a big hairy German Shepard dog with a welcoming smile on its face and a long tail wagging so much it was sweeping snow from the road. For that half a second though, it was a bloody wolf and my heart came up as my bowels went down. Once I'd recovered and was back in control, I felt comfort in the companionship. It was so amazing to have someone to chat with as I hadn't seen a living thing for hours, even if he didn't know what I was saying, because he was German and just kept looking up at me smiling. I stopped to examine Mutley - I call all dogs Mutley - to see if there was a collar, and for a cuddle. There wasn't a sign of any ownership and, with a thorough examination of my surroundings realising there was no one else around, I decided there was nothing I could do but march on with Mutley moseying along next to me. An hour and a half of chatting away with Mutley, wishing and hoping I now had this friend with me for the entirety of the race and imagining sharing a cuddle in the tent to keep each other warm at night, a skidoo came crunching up next to us. The local guy on it was shouting and smiling, 'there's me dog' in a very strong Canadian accent that I barely understood. As soon as Mutley recognised its owner, he became playful and started prancing around trying to entice us to catch her. Disconnecting myself from my sled I joined the owner in a bit of cat and mouse until I attracted my furry friend with a bit of food, enabling its capture and entrapment into a trailer on the back of the skidoo. With a shake of the hands and a few words from the owner that I didn't quite understand, I was left back in my world of nothingness. Although this time, the isolation felt more lonely, so I slowed down until Rio joined me for some company and someone to share my story with.

We checked into the Tombstone Campground together in first and second place at approximately 10pm, eleven and a half hours after the gun was fired. The plan was to grab food, get three hours sleep and head straight to the top of Tombstone Mountain together, the highest part of the Dempster Highway, feeling totally in control and miles ahead of anyone else. The checkpoint was freezing. As the night had closed in, the temperature dropped to around minus 25 degrees Celsius, much colder than the unseasonably warm minus 10 degrees Celsius we had during the day. With it being such a warm day, it actually caused problems. We weren't set up for it, so keeping the sweating to a minimum was a constant issue. The shelter had no lights or heating, making efficiency the key, so after a very productive three hours sleep, I managed to completely get dressed inside the sleeping bag within a minute or two. Then eagerly smashed down four packets of porridge, along with a jar of nitrous-fuelled coffee, and I was ready to perform. Standing by the exit, raring to disappear into the darkest, most intimidating night I have ever seen, I looked around to find Rio was still munching on food and repacking his sled. I was starting to shiver because I was dressed for moving, not standing, so instructing him to catch me up, I took a breath and began once again to take it one step at a time out of the security of the lodge and into a claustrophobic darkness.

The next section was said to be some of the hardest miles of the race which I definitely felt within a few metres of leaving the camp. The route just went vertical, and the climb to the top of Tombstone was unexpectedly steep. The climb would have been difficult enough on its own, without the dark, the minus 25 degrees, the thirty-kilo sled hanging from my hips, and the understanding that sweat is dangerous in this environment. So many athletes have needed to withdraw from races like this because their clothes had frozen on them, causing a world of hyperthermic problems. It wasn't long before I had sweat dripping from my nose, running down my back and soaking all my layers. I decided I had two options: one, get changed quickly into a new set of dry clothes from the sled and take it a bit easier, or march like I'd nicked the sled, keep my temperature up as high as I could and get to the top, then deal with the wet clothing as quick as possible. I moved like I was possessed, climbing up and over Tombstone at such a speed I had created around a three-hour lead on Rio and a further three hours on anyone else in the race by the time the dawn broke. The problem was, I was now heading downhill, and the temperature had dropped further to minus 30 degrees Celsius, and in damp clothes I had entered into an uncontrollable shake. It was time to mentally go over how I was going to fix this problem and then put it into action. Running through the As, Bs and Cs of the next few minutes a couple of times in my head, I stopped then proceeded as planned with the utmost urgency, grabbing food and a hot drink whilst stripping and reclothing with the speed of a formula one pit crew. I just about accomplished the challenge before my hands became useless with no dexterity whatsoever; painful and frigid. I tried all the tricks I could to re-warm them so I could finish the pit-stop and continue on my way. They couldn't move a zip, open a packet of hand warmers, or grasp hold of my warm cup of coffee. I even struggled for five minutes to press the emergency button on the sled to ask for help, which could technically mean I was out of the race. With my jacket still undone and too much skin showing, I was slightly panicking, resorting to sprinting up and down the road for thirty minutes until help came. Fortunately, when the crew arrived, they let me guide my hands through a half-opened window of the 4x4 and proceeded to rub them until feeling came back and I was able to finish packing and dressing. They did warn me that any further assistance and I would be out of the race.

Checkpoint 2 was just a large trailer parked on the side of the road eighty-two miles from the start line. It was now 4 ish in the afternoon, so approaching thirty hours of racing. This was just a quick and simple checkpoint with no luxuries, just some warmth and food, and with a space off the road to pitch my tent. Arriving there a few hours in front of Rio and eight hours in front of anyone else, I still felt reasonably ok apart from struggling with cold damage on my hands. Pitching my tent was a major operation with hands that weren't user friendly and fell apart as soon as they felt the slightest cold. After multiple visits into the warm van to bring them back to life, I managed to get the tent up and I was nicely cosy in my sleeping bag trying to get some zzzzz. Just as I was about to hit a deep sleep, I woke up startled and restricted with what I thought was a panic attack. My breathing started to gurgle, and I felt like I was choking as if I was trying to recover from being waterboarded. Every inhaled breath was loose, and every out breath was an unrelenting cough. Looking back, I realised it was because of the condensation in the tent that had been created from my body heat. Later, I was told that If I'd left the zip half open, I would have been fine. That little nugget of information would have been a little better received when I was crawling into the van on my hands and knees for the first time gasping for air. It wasn't long before I could breathe again, though, and I was trying once more to get some sleep. Repeating the process of not being able to breathe and crawling to the van to recover three times, and having hands that couldn't pull the zip up on the sleeping bag, I gave up and slept in the 4x4. Unfortunately, I realised when I woke up that this decision eliminated me from the race.

All these problems were totally preventable and all down to my inexperience. I was, as you can imagine, totally gutted. Gutted for myself because I had earned the right to be here this time. Gutted for everyone following me and supporting me. But, most of all, gutted for Teri and the girls. They had put up with so much from me; mood swings, tiredness and constantly being disengaged. We had lost precious time together; they had sacrificed their own interests and missed out on opportunities because of my devotion to finishing this chapter of my life, and not to mention the financial burden a race like this puts on a family. This was all I could think about during the three days it took me to get home.

Walking into our house, the atmosphere was flat. Teri was as emotional about this as me, probably more so. I was in the driver's seat of the whole charade, and Teri was unfortunately a passenger who felt helpless and out of control. She was feeling every discomfort and bump in the road I was but had no way of connecting with the pain. She suffered every mile, every early morning, every bit of isolation, and every bit of gut-wrenching disappointment as I did, but had no release from it. There was a little distance between us, and the house as a unit, for a few weeks. It was like the house was grieving. I know it sounds a bit dramatic, but this was such a big part of the past couple of years.

Life felt a bit empty, for me at least. As always though, time is a great healer and I started to realise, in a way, I hadn't failed the race. I'd just not finished the victory lap. Once the dust had settled, I felt more refreshed and more rejuvenated than I had felt for years. I would nearly go as far as saying I was excited about the future. Understanding that absolutely everything that was possible to be done, had been done, to prepare for such a massive, overwhelming and intimidating obstacle. It was defining and it was rewarding in itself. I felt I had been successful in the challenge; I just didn't finish. I'd done the training, acquired the right equipment, researched every possible piece of literature, and had become resilient and stoic. Physically and mentally I still believe I absolutely nailed that race. I had completed my transformation. I had completed the morph from the overweight, egotistical, smoking, drinking, selfish individual, to the healthy, active, successful, energetic and dependable partner and father. I absolutely rose to the challenge, but just didn't get a medal at the end of it.

I honestly didn't feel the need, or the attraction, to compete anymore. My renewed energy was spent on family time, holidays and work. My clients received all of me again for the first time in years. My training reduced to a normal level of an hour a day, mostly lifting weights with my mates and daughters. I enjoyed the summer on my motorbike and walking the dogs. Life was starting to feel balanced. I nearly felt normal, for a few months anyway, but then as always, my darkness started eclipsing the brightness. Work was getting heavy again, normality was becoming constrictive, multiple voices were trying to hurt me. My insides were being squeezed, and at times I couldn't take a deep breath. I needed to find space - space from my own thoughts and emotions. I needed a holiday from me again. WHAT THE FUCK? BOLLOCKS. Why can't I just be bloody normal? AAAHHHH.

It was like the universe was listening, because just as I was going through all the options of how I would deal with my fucking head, options like, shall I book another stupid race, or shall I get counselling; maybe drugs are the answer or changing my career. I was even considering moving to Cornwall. An email vibrated through my watch with the title '6633 Arctic Ultra, 2022 entrances are now open with big discounts'. Standing against the kitchen counter waiting for the kettle to boil, I opened that bloody email knowing it would make the next six months inevitably predictable. This was the equivalent of tempting an alcoholic with one more drink. After all, what damage can one drink do? Just one last time, you'll be fine! Reading the email, there it was, a massive discount for competitors who competed in the experimental 250-mile race of 2021 to say thank you for keeping the company alive. This was going to be the first time in three years that the official 383-mile 6633 Arctic Ultra was going ahead, and it was going to be epic, with some big names competing. Shiiiit, shit, shit, and I was off - 'first drink consumed'. What damage can just one drink do? I can tell you right now, the first drink is fucking dangerous, can cause a lot of damage; and I promise you, it most definitely will not be fine.

Chapter 3

One Breath, One Step, One Second At A Time!

One breath, one step, one second at a time! Is there any other way to start, partake in and finish a journey?

We are all on a journey. From our biological creation to our inevitable death. Some say it's a long, educational and spiritual journey, whilst others tell us life is short and disappears in the blink of an eye. One thing is definite whichever way you look at it, it can only be taken one breath, one step and one second at a time.

Unfortunately, most of us try impossibly to live the whole journey, all the time, as we consistently repeat decisions we have already made in our mind, trying to justify it was the right decision, or wishing we could have made a different choice now we have some new knowledge. Obviously, this is impossible because regardless of how clever Doc and Marty are in 'Back to The Future', you can't go back in time. It's the inaccessibility of the already-trodden part of your journey, and the understanding that we cannot change it that causes stress. Trying to relive past seconds instead of looking after *this* second and then *this* second, is the first mistake that contributes to mental health issues. Letting the past dictate the present is a problem we are all guilty of as we continually hold ourselves in contempt for being such an ass.

Equally, we are all becoming scared little rabbits in the oncoming headlights of time as we force predicted outcomes on our unpredictable future selves. Leaving ourselves frozen in time because we daren't take a step in any direction in case it's the wrong direction, and we get run over by the imaginary vehicle we've predicted could be careering towards us. Trying to live in the future seconds, minutes, days and years of our journey stops us living at all in the present, and creates the anxiety pit we have all fallen into recently.

Second by second is the only way to travel through our journey. Living outside this simple reality, creating past and future realities has become, more than ever, an issue that is preventing progress, adaptation and growth. It's stopping us showing empathy towards each other because someone might not want it. It's stopping community spirit as we are driven to stay in the security of individual space just in case, we might offend someone by calling them the wrong pronoun. It's creating a world where humans can't be human. The human spirit is dying, and I blame, in part, social media for its constant bombardment of everyone else's past mistakes and predicted futures. We can't confidently make a choice about anything anymore without being shown possible outcomes of what will happen if you make this decision, or that decision on a political vote, a holiday destination, a career choice, or even an item of clothing you were thinking of wearing for a special occasion. It cleverly keeps us in the world of stress and anxiety, creating massive weights of depression on our shoulders by repeatedly feeding us the past wrongdoings and future predictions.

The power of living second by second is too overwhelming for most, and in all honesty very hard to maintain. We find comfort in living in the past as we can more easily show anger and misfortune in something we can't change, so there is no pressure to do anything about it. Living in a future world is also a self-preservation tactic because we can't act on a situation if it hasn't happened yet, once again creating something that isn't our fault. But when the shit really hits the fan, when things really turn into a life-or-death situation, the second you are feeling right now is the only second you are thinking about. Things that have happened in the past are irrelevant as well as predicted scenarios of the future - who bloody cares?

There have been a few instances I can quickly recall from my life that have forced me to count the passing seconds, and only the passing seconds. The worst experience I went through was when we nearly lost our youngest daughter shortly after she was born. Three days after her birth she was luckily seen by my mother-in-law turning blue from reflux which was blocking her airways. They said it was reflux at the time, but we knew there was something more sinister behind it. Once the airways were cleared and normal breathing returned, she was taken to hospital where she spent the next few days losing weight, unable to keep anything down, not even water. A week after her day of birth she had lost a third of her body weight whilst living on a drip and having test after test performed on her as they tried to understand what was wrong. The worst noise you will ever hear is your baby screaming in pain to the extent they can no longer breathe properly, as you stand by helplessly in a hospital hallway feeling every single prod, poke and needle your cherished loved one feels from the doctors as they continuously look for answers that will keep her alive. I guarantee that any emotional connection to the past or future had disappeared at this point as they had become totally insignificant. Past worries gone, financial worries gone, career worries gone, even mental illness issues gone. Everything else apart from that second was gone. You are basically sitting on the plastic seat for hour after hour totally connected with every single second that ticks by on the clock facing you on the hospital wall, praying that they figure it out before the clock stops and there are no more seconds left.

Situations like that really make you live in the moment. The very second, we found out they knew what the problem was, that they had a plan for how to correct it, and that she was going to be fine almost immediately after the necessary treatment, was the happiest second of my life. That single inhalation and exhalation of breath in that moment was the deepest, longest and most detoxing release of breath I can say I have ever felt. In that one breath, a week's worth of stress, anxiety, exhaustion, gut-wrenching tension and hopelessness disappeared. In that one breath, in that one second, my overpowering stress hormones were instantly replaced by endorphins, serotonin and dopamine; all the hormones that make you overjoyed and uplifted that allow the healing to start. Unfortunately, that release of air from your lungs, that one breath, stops you living in the present and instantly sends you back to contemplating what could have happened, and how the future would look if things had gone the other way. Our coping strategies strangely propel us back to alternative realities.

If we can nurture the power we have when shit hits the fan to live in the moment, and use it when there's less shit, or no shit, or possibly when really good shit is happening, we would spend less time in the past and the future. If we could relearn how to use our breath as a release of tension, much like when a horse yawns after going past an object it was nervous about passing, or a dog deeply exhales whilst shaking off the tension of a confrontation with another dog. If we can build a habit of taking and giving one big deep breath before stepping forward into the unknown or the unwanted, it would give us power and bring us back to the present. That single breath will allow us to have that moment of clarity we need to take us away from the alternate realities we have manifested in our screwed-up minds, allowing the true reality to feel a hell of a lot easier. After all, once you've triumphed over it, you only have to deal with this reality one single second at a time, then just deal with the next one. Before long, you start becoming a master of only challenging, conquering and living life one second at a time, and not suffering from the anxiety of trying to predict the endless scenarios of future events whilst making plans on how to stay safe in each one of them.

We were told my daughter probably only had a day left in her when they discovered the problem at the hospital. It turned out that she had Pyloric Stenosis. This is a condition where the valve that allows food and drink to pass from the stomach into the intestines becomes overgrown, preventing her from absorbing or digesting anything, so it was the regurgitation of the gloopy milk that kept blocking her airways. A small operation to cut away the overgrowth and she was as right as rain.

Breath is the most valuable resource we have. It releases tension, gives you clarity, provides a rhythm in life and contributes to your strength. Controlling it, feeling it, and consciously connecting with it will bring balance, power, contentment, health and freedom. Obviously, we all breathe, but how many of us think about breathing? How many of us practise breathing techniques through mediation, breath holding, burst breathing, and other practices, enabling control and efficiency of our breath and using it with purpose. This might sound absurd when you consider you've been breathing very well since the day you were born, but have you? Practising controlled breathing and understanding its strength has so many health benefits.

I have spent some time in the past few years studying a guy called Wim Hof, who's also known as the Ice Man because of his remarkable capabilities of cold weather endurance. He has, among other achievements, conquered Everest in his shorts, holds the world record of sixty-six meters for the longest swim with a single breath under arctic ice water, run an arctic half marathon barefoot and in shorts, and spent nearly two hours in an ice bath whilst maintaining a normal body temperature. He masters all this through breathing techniques, meditation and regular extreme cold exposure. His book called 'The Wim Hof Method' explains how and why his methods help with all aspects of mental and physical health, contributing to unbelievable amounts of strength, resistance, and determination. I won't dilute his teachings by trying to explain them here, but just say it's very easy to follow and will help you achieve goals, grow in ways you never thought you needed, and help you find balance with yourself and your surroundings.

I practise his teachings as often as I can, and when I find I don't have the time or the drive to set aside some time for it, I force myself to do it more. Fifteen to twenty minutes a day is all it takes to change the way I approach life, keeping me calm and focused while building belief in self.

Walking meditation is something I picked up from Mikey, a good friend of mine whom I previously mentioned in the first book. Most days I try to include a little presence into my daily walks with the dog, and if I'm particularly struggling. I'll venture out specifically for a twenty-minute meditation around the tarmac of my hometown. It doesn't matter where you are; it could be strolling through the local park or fields, around the block, or even just repeatedly doing laps of your own garden. It starts by relaxing the whole body as you move forward, slowly feeling the connection with the ground with each step as it rolls from heel to toe until eventually you feel a gliding sensation. Concentrate on the movement in the ankle as its flexibility increases with each strike of the ground, then move your concentration up to the knees and the hips as you feel the joints doing what they are built to do, and the muscles creating stability. Even feel the slight sway from one side of your core to the other as your centre of gravity swings with each step. Let the arms naturally move in relation to your stride to maintain momentum, then slightly tilt your head forward and extend the neck, opening the airwaves, before you start counting your steps like a metronome. Once all of this starts to link together and you feel at one with your surroundings, and a little at peace with yourself, start connecting your steps with your breath. Breath in for two steps and out for two steps, in for two steps and out for two steps. After a minute or so, and once a rhythm has been established, go for four steps. Breathing in for four steps and out four steps. After another minute or two, increase to six in and out. Continue increasing the steps by two more every minute or so until it becomes difficult to continue, and you start to struggle with it. This is when the magic happens; this is when you learn self-control as you try to reduce the panic reflex and consciously try to relax your heart rate, whilst maintaining a very slow inhale and exhale rhythm. Hopefully you will have reached around twelve, fourteen or even sixteen strides on an inbreath and then matching it on the out breath. Struggle through the discomfort, even start to feel the control and peace in the activity and challenge yourself to connect with your own uneasiness. After a few long, slow breaths at your limit, start reducing the steps related to each breath, holding the new rhythm of ten in and out for a minute or so, then to eight in and out, and six, four and finally two. Repeat the cycle as many times as you can or feel content with. Just try the cycle once to start with and then, as confidence and connection builds, increase your willingness to improve.

This teaches the acceptance of discomfort without panicking. When life throws you a curveball, know that you can take a breath, assess the situation and step forward. Standing like a rabbit in the headlights with your heart racing, unable to make a decision through fear, isn't going to make anyone's day better. Acceptance, self-discipline, control and direction is what you achieve when you learn how to breathe efficiently and consciously.

You can also use a breath to accept pain or push through a painful or uncomfortable situation. Ant Middleton, an ex-SAS soldier and TV celebrity, describes the use of the fear bubble in his book called 'The Fear Bubble'. Once again, he explains better than me how he used the concept of the fear bubble to stop him ruining large parts of his life through fear. During a period of leave he would spend a large chunk of his time living in fear before heading back to a war zone. He would spend the last few days living with a knot in his guts anticipating his return to work, destroying those last precious days with his family. One morning

Ant was sitting with his freshly brewed coffee in his comfortable family home, sweating with anxiety at the thought of going back to Afghanistan and trying to find a way of dealing with it. This is when he came up with the fear bubble concept. Looking around his home, which was full of support and love in the relatively safe environment of middle England, he changed his thought processes to understand that this isn't the time or place to feel 'the fear'. Let's save it until I am on the plane and actually heading to the area that produced the fear. That is when I will allow myself to feel the fear, he told himself. So, with a deep breath in, and a long slow breath out, he snapped himself out of it. Days later when he was on the return flight to Afghanistan, he realised this isn't the time to feel the fear either. He looked around and acknowledged he was on a commercial flight being fed and watered whilst watching a movie along with all the other comfortable civilians, so he decided to delay the fear further. After a deep breath to release the tension, he justified that the fear should be allowed to show itself when he arrived at Base Camp, then relaxed into the flight. Base Camp arrived and he was welcomed back by all his brothers in arms with pats on the back, big hugs, barbecued food and a few beers. With another breath of relief, he decided he was safe and so relaxed himself into a fun evening. Later he understood there was nothing to actually feel fearful about until we were sent on a mission, when we're in the air heading towards the war zone. But when this was the case and he was in the chopper, orders having been given and with a gun in his hand, he once again broke away from the fear when realising that there was still nothing to be scared of - yet. He was still safe. Even when he jumped out of the helicopter and walked the ten miles towards the village, they were supposed to take control of, he was still safe. In fact, there was no need to allow the fear in until the point when he briefly poked his head around the end of a wall in the village and saw, for the first time, an enemy soldier. This is it; this is the time to feel the fear. It was time to let it in and allow the essential hormones that get dumped into the bloodstream to keep you alert and ready to tackle the fearful moment. It's fear bubble time. He describes being able to visually see the bubble in front of him. At the end of that wall was the bubble. That was the location where fear could take control, and it was his choice when he would step into it. If he stepped into it and realised it was the wrong time, he could step out to gather himself before trying again. He would count to three, take a deep breath and blow it out slowly and in a controlled way as he stepped into the bubble once more. As soon as he'd taken the shot and the deed was done, the bubble would burst and he'd calm down, releasing the fear, allowing him to progress forward into the mission without carrying unnecessary stress. When he saw another bubble, he would deal with it in exactly the same way. One bubble at a time, he would progress through the mission dealing with bubble after bubble methodically and precisely.

Ant managed to break down the anxiety and stress of a truly terrifying situation, like war, from the initial torment of days upon days of fear that his family had to endure, whilst, supposedly, enjoying his annual leave, to a few seconds of high intensity dread and apprehension. This released him from the chains that bound him unnecessarily to an environment he wasn't currently in that was still in the future and gave him freedom to enjoy 99% of his life while dealing with the other 1% on his own terms.

This can be used in life to help with whatever possible situation you have to overcome that scares you. Any problem you are going through that is currently dominating every part of your day, just break it down, and keep breaking it down until you have a few seconds of a fear bubble. Taking an exam, going to the dentist, heading for a job interview, waiting for surgery, going out on a first date. Everything that has a premature hold on you can be broken down to seconds of fear or pain. The freedom felt from being in control of your fear and choosing when to feel it is empowering. See the bubble, count to three, take an empowering breath and release as you step into the bubble, do what needs to be done and relax. The breath is the deciding factor. The breath is what gives you the power.

Thankfully, I've never been to war or in a war zone, but I believe the biggest conflicts we all have to deal with are with ourselves. The arguments we constantly persist with on a daily basis are suffocating and possessive. This is another reason I feel addicted to races. It allows me to practise processing where I am right now; just, 'the now'. Racing helps me to build the muscles that deal with just the next step, not the whole journey. The whole journey is too scary and intimidating. One step at a time is the easiest way to get to the finish line. It's not the only way, but it's the least painful. You can battle through life trying to understand, anticipate and overcome your whole existence every single day, which is way too heavy, or you can spend most of your energy just dealing with the next step. What steps do I need to take today? A lot less of a burden to carry. Staring at my medals hanging on the wall opposite me, I instantly remember the races I finished whilst struggling through every mile, all at the same time, with every step taken; and they were bloody tough days, not enjoyable whatsoever. In fact, they were downright torturous. But the races I felt, dealt with, and overcame every step as it happened, were the events I proudly talk about. They were the challenges where I had time to lift my head to admire the scenery, feel my energy grow and be at one with myself for a few hours. They were a release from the tensions I normally carry, just because I was only caring about this step, this second and this breath. I've taken part in close to a hundred races and done twenty thousand miles of training, just in the last five years. I can't imagine how many steps that has been, but I know for a fact that most of them have been done consciously, taking it one step at a time. Combining the relationship of breathing in time with stepping forward has been so rewarding and helpful. I use it more often than I think. Daily I catch myself repeating, 'just take a breath and step forward'.

Even now I feel the need to take things a breath, a step and a second at a time because my eldest daughter has just left me in a self-pity hole as she set off travelling around the eastern countries for a few months with a couple of friends. I'm waking up every day feeling a part of me is missing. Her coat is hanging on the back of the door, so when I open it I can smell perfume. I know, I'm a soft old git, but I've been in charge of safety, education and nurture for all her twenty-two years, and within a second it was gone. How am I dealing with it? Well, I think you have the idea now.

Every journey, every life change within a lifetime, every challenge and every difficulty starts with a breath of acceptance. Every transition through fatherhood, adulthood, into retirement or change of career, maybe going through a divorce, or dealing with the loss of someone, can only be done by powering through ‘the now’. If you don’t and you try to deal with the whole problem, or carry all the emotions at once, nothing will be achieved, no progress will be made, because it’s far too big a picture to look at.

Practise the art of taking life one breath, one step and one second at a time. Whenever anything gets too much, or too painful, take a breath. Whenever you don’t know how to move on, take a step. Whenever life gives you shit, take it one second at a time, even if it's the good shit. Don't waste any of the good times worrying about anything else; just enjoy the second you’re feeling right now and roll with it.

Chapter 4
WTF?

Whitehorse … Again!

Hello Whitehorse. Fancy seeing you again so soon.

This is it. Ten years, nearly to the day, since I first laid my naive footsies on Canadian soil. A whole decade where I'd spent most of it changing absolutely everything about who I am and what I stand for. My personality, my career, my health, my finances, the impression I leave on others, and in the energy, I have with everyone around me; from my nearest and dearest, to the people just passing by. The evolution of Stu Humber has been memorable, and in a lot of ways, over such a relatively short period of time. I can only hope that the connections I have made with everyone are generally positive; but for me, this is the time to put all that to the test and close this chapter of my life.

My training and preparation for this has been faultless, and I've added some valuable, hard lessons throughout the last few years, not just for racing but for life. I'm even feeling confident about my hand issues. All in all, I couldn't have done a single thing more to assure my legs were going to walk onto the frozen Arctic Ocean in Tuktoyaktuk, or Tuk for short. A whole decade worth of studying, building, grinding sacrifice, development and progression, not just from me, but my family. It has given me the confidence and self-awareness to put this chapter in our life to bed. It's been a long time coming, and all of us need me to move on now. It's become a weight and a shadow that follows us all around. The whole family needs me to remove these chains so we can throw ourselves into this new life we have created.

I felt different this time. More in control, more confident, more present and more worthy. Before departing, I had decided I was going to keep myself a bit more isolated this time, make myself a bit of a lone wolf. I felt a disciplined energy that was comfortable but driven, and for the first time I already had the best wing man I could ask for - myself. I didn't need to be with anyone else. I hadn't felt so connected and balanced before, and I already knew I was going to finish. I knew that I was capable of taking on whatever the road, the race, the weather or the Arctic could throw at me, by following one simple rule: Take it one breath, one step, and one second at a time. Whatever happens, just deal with it a breath, a step and a second at a time. That way, box after box will get ticked off until there are no more boxes to be ticked, and I'm standing at the finish line in Tuk.

Proceedings from landing in Whitehorse to arriving at Eagle Plains and the start line of this unforgettable adventure went as scheduled. The usual shopping list was acquired, kit checks completed, meetings attended, chit chat and stories shared, and acquaintances made. I spent most of these few days quietly, but confidently, sitting in the corner, keeping myself to myself, soaking up everyone's energy and reading their expressive positives and negatives about the forthcoming activities.

Most of the twenty-eight strong competitors were showing the usual excited, jittery nervousness, apart from a special few that stood out: in my opinion anyway. Firstly Vlad; he was back, after finishing the 250-miler last year in second place, a few hours behind my companion at the start, Rio. Rio did outstandingly well last year. Not only was he the youngest-ever finisher of any 6633 event, but he won it. I wanted to verbally congratulate him, so I called him up in Canada to give him a congratulatory hug and pat on the back; well, you know what I mean. I was very proud of him, and we shared a lovely chat when he finished. He returned the compliment by giving me a nice homage by saying he felt it was my race, and I should have won. He also mentioned he very much struggled once he realised, I was out, because he had no one to chase. Admirable of him to say that, but in order to win anything, you have to finish it first.

Another athlete that caught my attention during the race prep was a young soldier called Tom. He also kept himself to himself and didn't seem to show the usual twitchiness of the others, especially as this was his first visit to the area. I felt an attraction to his energy that showed self-confidence and control. Then there was Natalie Taylor. She was constantly full of beans, very aware, and seemed to give the impression she was there for a party. Nothing swayed her bubbly approach to everything, making her a pleasure to be around. Natalie was very accepted by all of us as well as the event crew, as her athletic reputation preceded her. I later discovered she was the favourite to win, and her nickname was the Ice Queen. Not for her icy demeaner, but because she had finished and smashed every cold weather event she had participated in. Her trophy cabinet, apart from being a Major in the Army, consisted of wins at the 50- and 100- mile Arc of Attrition race that ran in January around the coastal path of Cornwall, and a win at the Ultra Tour De Monte Rosa staged race. Two Iron Man competitions thirteen days apart, along with second places at the Glencoe Skyline and the Ultra Trail Great Britain 215-mile race. None of these are races that even experienced ultra runners take lightly. She was also part of an all-woman expedition that crossed the South Pole over forty-seven days, covering 944 km. I would confidently say that the rest of us were competing for second place. My old mate Mal was also with us for a couple of weeks away from home. At 70-ish years old, he was still making it through the 120-mile race, and that's with a couple of hip replacements. An outstanding achievement and a lovely guy.

The big morning arrived. As I turned the corner into the restaurant area, it was the usual feeding time at the zoo as everyone was stuffing their faces with every calorie, they could grab hold of. The Eagle Plains truck stop always provided such a wonderful breakfast to set us up for the day. Whilst tucking into my dustbin-lid-sized plate of greasy food, I could hear the rumours of a huge storm that was supposed to be crossing Canada. Its projected path was going to hit our route a little north from here at some point in the next twenty-four hours and was capable of causing the area some issues. 'Some issues' isn't a phrase that should be taken lightly in this environment. Where I come from, some issues could mean a few tree branches falling onto the roads or the danger of some flooding here and there. 'Some issues' here means 50-60 mph snow blizzards and minus 30 degree Celsius temperatures creating wind chills entering the -70's. Visibility will be non-existent, and any exposed skin will get destroyed in minutes. It turned out that this wasn't just a rumour; this was coming, and it was highly likely we'd be seeing it. The event crew felt the need to pull us all together to go over a few more safety issues and advised us to hit the ground running as soon as the gun fired in an attempt to get north of the storm before it hit.

Trouble ... again!

As instructed, and with the expected, but always surprisingly loud BANG from the pistol pointed skyward, we were off, heading north on the Dempster Highway. 383 miles of blood, sweat and tears, fortunes and misfortunes, barriers to break through and new paths to create. Even though we all set off together, we were all, really, just racing ourselves with our own individual challenges, and trying to beat whatever obstacle it was we imagined was in front us. The scheduled route would take us first to Fort Mcpherson, 113 miles up the highway and checkpoint 3. This is where we jumped onto an ice road for a further 173 miles to Inuvik, checkpoint 6. Concluding with another road section of 97 miles that would sweep us all the way to checkpoint 8 and to the frozen ocean in Tuktoyaktuk. 383 miles of surprises, -20 to -40 degrees Celsius, blizzards and sunshine, totally self-sufficient and reliant on our own survival capabilities.

Leaving Eagle Plains, the weather was already a bit grim. The thermostat was already showing well below -20 and the wind was starting to blow nicely. Skin needed to be covered immediately, as I was sternly warned to cover up during the first ten miles of the race, because my cheeks were already showing signs of future cold damage. This was already proving to be a hell of a race. The Arctic circle sign appeared on my right, twenty-three miles, and five and a half hours into the race. I was in third position behind Natalie and Tom, and they were both in view with Natalie edging the lead. The temperature was holding steady, but the wind was building. I was slightly sweaty from the climb up and out of the Yukon and was now entering the hills where the Northwest Territories began. The next 50-ish miles rolled along this very hilly section called Snake Pass or Hurricane Alley, whatever name you want to use to intimidate listeners of your future stories. The katabatic winds arrive and disappear, often without warning, and can easily blow over the trucks up there.

Heading down into a valley, the wind eased, giving some respite and some time to assess. Still comfortably in third place a few hundred metres behind the two leaders who were now walking together, we edged closer to Checkpoint 1. This checkpoint was at the base of the valley forty-two miles from the start and away from the surrounding bad weather. It was, however, just a large trailer attached to a 4x4, which meant no creature comforts, just water and a chair. Entering the trailer a few minutes later than the leaders, I managed to get the tail end of a conversation, and the news that was going to drastically change the race. The storm that was passing in front of us had already dumped quite a few feet of snow causing an avalanche. This covered the road about twenty miles away and was unpassable. Also, another avalanche had rolled over a section of road we had just passed, back in the Yukon. We were basically stuck inside a 40-mile section of highway until snow ploughs could cut through and release us. ‘Shit’ was probably the politest word that entered my head. Anything can happen in this environment and most of the time it does. A new plan was needed, and quickly.

The road ahead was clear and accessible for around fifteen miles, as was the road behind, all the way to the Arctic Circle sign, roughly seventeen miles away. The plan was to continue forward for fifteen miles where there would be a crewed vehicle to turn us back to checkpoint 1. Then, fingers crossed, the road would be clear, and we would be forwarded on the fifteen miles we'd have covered walking back towards this checkpoint. Sounded clear and easy to follow. With that, I decided to pitch my tent, get some food, grab ninety minutes of sleep, reset and continue up the highway, hopefully a bit fresher. The leading 2 decided to continue on up to Hurricane Alley, stretching their lead.

A couple of hours later, and ready for another thirty miles, I inhaled some more food and went after the leaders. The unfortunate thing about being trapped here though was the hills. This was the part of the race with all of the elevation, at least 80% of it anyway. The legs and hips felt the inclines almost immediately. Everyone was dealing with the same issues though, so it was a case of suck it up and take it one step at a time. The winds were back as soon as I peeked on one of the hills but made yesterday's winds feel like a breeze; and to add to this, snow was now joining the party. Within a few hours visibility became near impossible, but I did see some light ahead and was hoping it was the turning point. I'd been out for a while but had no idea how far I had travelled. My hopes continued to increase as I stared at that light, praying for the turnaround. I felt complete exhaustion from the battle of each step in those winds, hills and the heavy snow. Unfortunately, it wasn't long before I became aware that the lights were moving up and down and side to side. It wasn't the turnaround vehicle at all; it was Natalie's and Tom's head torches. They came into view looking like they'd been in a frozen washing machine, not a millimetre of skin showing, clothing all dishevelled, and covered in ice and snow. Through shaky voices they warned me, "put every item of clothing you have on now; it's terrible up there". As their lights faded away behind me, they shouted back, "It's just another five miles until the turnaround point, stay safe". Five miles, five more bloody miles, and I thought I was nearly there; I'd been gone for hours. I couldn't change this fact though, so it was head down and get on with it. I took their advice and kitted up before heading higher up the hill. Not a single piece of skin was showing, and I felt like a walking wardrobe.

They weren't exaggerating. Within fifteen minutes the weather turned completely bonkers. I had no idea where I was or in what direction I was walking, and I could feel the intensity of the snow impacting me through the numerous layers of clothing. The wind was forcing me to walk sideways in the hope I could travel even slightly forward. I couldn't even see my feet, and the sled was being blown sideways in the opposite direction as I was trying to move. It must have been a couple of hours of struggle, fight, and, basically, torture before I thought I heard a voice shout my name in the distance. I couldn't see anything, and the sound was so faint, it could have even been the wind or my imagination, so I just fought on. Then it came again. I heard someone shout "Stu", more abruptly this time. "Who's that I screamed? Where are you?" "It's Jonny, mate", came a distant response. "Where are you Jonny?" I desperately wailed. "Reach your hand out to the left", he said. Reaching out I felt him grab my wrist and pull me to the side of the 4x4. "You ok Stu?", he asked. "I think the wind's picked up a touch mate, is this the turnaround", I asked "We've come forward three more miles; It's too nasty further on. Just turn around and head back, bud. It's too dangerous". I didn't need telling twice.

The twelve miles back to checkpoint 1 took around five hours. I passed most of the other athletes heading into hell and gave them the same warning I had received. The last two racers I met before the safety of the trailer were the two leaders starting their second loop. I guessed if they were travelling back out again, we must still be stuck on our own little distant planet, miles away from civilization. Receiving confirmation of this at the checkpoint, I decided to grab another couple of hours of sleep and took time to refuel before thinking about heading back out, mainly because I was actually a little scared. It was terrifying out there, and the thought of facing it again sent a different type of chill down my spine.

The weather was calmer when I woke up around midday, the storm had passed, but I was told we were still stuck. Everyone who wasn't asleep in their tents was on the out and back to the 12-mile turnaround point. Grabbing some breakfast in the trailer and talking to the crew, they decided to make it a little more interesting for me. "Let's send you back to the Arctic Circle sign", they thought out loud. "When you've done the 17-mile hike to the top, there'll be someone there to check on you before sending you back here", they continued. "Okie dokie", I replied, and went out to efficiently pack my home away so I could eagerly add a few more miles to my tally. It was a refreshingly lovely, crispy afternoon with blue skies, and the temperature was comfortably back into the relative warmth of minus 15 degrees. The going was tough, though. The storm had dumped five to six inches of fresh virgin snow on the road, which made pulling the sled up the 2,000 feet of elevation hard. It wasn't long before an old injury flared up; the injury I suffered when I was first here ten years ago and was given a really crap sled. That sled destroyed my hip, making me unable to walk properly for weeks and incapable of running for months.

I hit the Arctic Circle sign in the darkness, dragging my left leg behind me as I winced in pain every time I relied on it for support. Once again, it was Jonny who greeted me through the window of the truck. I explained to him my pain and inability to continue in the race, to which he sternly replied "Don't give me any of that shit. Get your tent up, get some food and get some rest. If you still want to be a quitter when you get back down to the checkpoint, I'll kick you out myself". Then with bullets in his eyes, he continued with, "I'm not taking your fucking arse down there. If you want to get off this mountain, you'll have to get down it yourself". He always knew what I needed to hear. Guessing this discussion was obviously finished, I erected my tent and shuffled inside. Crying in pain as I slid into my sleeping bag, and whilst eating some sugary treats I had left in there from the night before, I slowly drifted in and out of consciousness. I heard athlete after athlete pass my tent, turn around and head back down, sending me further and further down the rankings. A few hours passed before I heard Jonny's voice call to me saying he was heading back now because the last of the racers had made the turn. If I needed help, then press the panic button. The panic button alerts the crew that I'm done and out of the race and is attached to my sled. Now Jonny had woken me up, I needed a pee, but my hip had further seized up. The only thing for it was to empty my flask of hot water and pee into the flask, which I surprisingly managed without spilling a drop, and then I dropped back off to sleep.

Waking up suddenly, I noticed it was now daylight again and the day sounded very calm. One thing I felt that was not calm was my stomach. The loud gurgling and rumbling noises were only matched by the excruciating cramps. These cramps were telling me something was coming whether I liked it or not and shitting in the sleeping back was definitely a no-no, especially as it wasn't mine. Counting to three I sat up, and with a sudden sharp crack from my hip it was mobile again; painful, but mobile. I didn't have time to enjoy a single moment of the now-free hip as something urgent was coming. I exited that tent like a greyhound out the gate, trousers down, and then Niagara Falls, although not so pleasant. Lovely, just fucking lovely, I thought. Another issue I've now got to deal with.

Once cleaned up and everything packed away, I remembered what my friend Mikey said to me before I left. "Lift your head every now and then to absorb where you are", so I did. It was stunning. It was actually the very first time I could see further than my nose. I felt on top of the world, not a single man-made object anywhere in sight. Pure nature at its artistic best. This view was nearly worth the price tag in itself, but unfortunately it was time to get this show back on road. Come on ya little bastard, I enthusiastically shouted to myself out loud at the top of my voice. Nobody was around to hear me, so why the hell not? I guessed I was probably in last place, but with my hip back on my side and the freshness of a lovely crisp morning, I felt motivated. That was until I needed another Niagara

Falls a few miles down the road, and then another and another. The only benefit of being miles from anyone is you can squat wherever you want. I didn't even detach from the sled the third time. Unfortunately, the repeated wiping was making me sore and it wasn't helping my dehydration as I'd emptied the last flask of water through the night to pee into. The struggle got worse, the discomfort grew and the dizziness became more frequent. With only a mile before the checkpoint, I must have walked straight off the raised highway as I found myself head down and arse up in the snow with my sled next to me upside down and with a very angry ankle. Frustrated, and now once again pissed off with the chain of events this race was throwing at me, I forcefully rearranged myself, and the sled, then limped to the checkpoint.

When I walked into that bloody checkpoint 'again' the only thing that stopped me quitting was the news that the road was now clear, and within minutes all the athletes would be collected wherever they were along the 'there and back' routes. Distances would be recorded and added to their totals before being taken to checkpoint 3, Fort Mcpherson, 113 miles from the start. We would all then have a two-hour recess to sort ourselves out, clean ourselves up and reset, while the event crew came up with a new plan.

Fort Mcpherson is one of the best checkpoints as well as the finish line for those who were taking part in the short version of the race, the 120. The local school provides the accommodation, and it was a much-needed break from the last couple of days. At this point, witnessing the state of not just the athletes but the crew, made me realise I wasn't alone in my misfortunes. The reception area was packed with shadows of what used to be people. It wasn't just the frostbite or the cuts and bruises, torn muscles or twisted joints, it was the gaunt look on everyone's face. No one would even lift their heads, never mind try to speak. The whole room was beaten, but after the two-hour recess, which would be taken off everyone's finishing time, some heads started to lift, and stories of events were starting to be told. At the end of the two-hours we all gathered back into the reception to hear the new plan.

From here, the race should have gone onto the ice road for approximately 180 miles, but unfortunately the storm had destroyed the whole of the man-made ice road. The entire 180 miles of road didn't exist anymore, and it wasn't going to be remade because it would only be a few weeks until it would melt in the spring. A new route to Inuvik needed to be made; they just didn't quite know how to do it yet. All they knew was where to place the next checkpoint, and once you arrived there, they would tell you where the next checkpoint was. The only thing they guaranteed was that we would still finish in Tuktoyaktuk and would still have covered 383 miles to get there. With that, we all got dressed back into our racing gear and were dropped at different locations along the route, depending on mileage covered whilst yo-yoing over the last couple of days. This is the point where my suspicions were confirmed. I was, in fact, in last place and still needed to cover another fifteen miles before officially arriving at the third checkpoint. I say last place; I was in fifteenth position because thirteen athletes had unfortunately already DNFd.

Sitting in the back of one of the American trucks, my anxiety increased when I realised how far away, I was from everyone else, and the fact I was about to be dumped at the side of the road on my own in the pitch black at 8pm. This felt worse because I was still sore from the diarrhoea, I had a stiff hip from the previous night in the tent, and I now had a nice cut and bruise on my ankle from falling off the road. I discovered this when I tried to take my sock off at the school, and the blood had glued the sock to the outside of my ankle. I departed the vehicle at the bottom of a steep valley, which firstly needed climbing out of. Standing there, watching the taillights disappear, I felt a 'fuck it' creeping in. Not a fuck it, I'm done and I'm out of here, but a 'fuck it', this race is mine. I hadn't put up with all this shit for nothing. Earphones went in and I started marching with intent, even jogging down the hills. I think this is the point Melvin took over and I took a back seat. Melvin is the name I give my monkey brain; my hypothalamus, which is the part of the brain that controls hormones and moods. This is our second voice that keeps us safe and alive and takes control whenever our rational thinking brain cannot cope with a situation. I was in such a hole that I couldn't rationalise it, so Melvin took the driving seat. I do love it when Melvin takes over because shit gets done. To the surprise of the crew, I officially arrived back at Fort Mcpherson before 11pm in eleventh position, as they asked if I had run the whole way back. "No, I'm just a bit pissed off!" I replied.

After first stuffing myself with food, then grabbing a good five hours sleep and shovelling more food down, I was standing at the exit of the school at 6am, being told where the next checkpoint would be. It was going to be the good old faithful trailer which we've all grown to love/hate, and it was going to be sitting on the Mackenzie River next to a small town called Tsiigehtchic some thirty-eight miles away. Martin, the race director, went on giving directions. "Go to the end of this road, turn left and keep going until you see the trailer". Even I could handle those directions.

With Melvin still in the driving seat, I was gone without the usual formalities that would coincide with leaving a CP. I was now emotionally separate from the activity. A job needed doing and that was that. I'd overcome the worst situation this race had ever encountered in its fourteen years, a damaged hip, smashed ankle and a sore arse from twelve hours of the shits. I was leaving in ninth place with thirty-eight miles in front of me and the promise of blue skies, still air and a comfortable minus 20-22 degrees Celsius, I was on the up and feeling optimistic. Game on.

The daylight came after a few hours. The skies were blue as the sun began to raise its head on the horizon. It was a lovely day, and for the first time I was happy to be here; I had found my racing legs. I was off, chasing down the next athlete who would come into my cross hairs. One by one I'd surge past them trying to make chit chat, but nothing was coming back from them; something was wrong. They all ignored me, giving me the cold shoulder. I didn't understand why, what had I done? Surely, they weren't pissed off just because I was passing them. I later found out that Vlad was spreading rumours about me getting help from the support crew and maybe even a lift, and of course everyone was believing this. Don't you just love human nature sometimes? Vlad was currently in third place, a good fifty miles behind the leading pair of Natalie and Tom who were setting an unprecedented pace. I had just moved into fourth position, moving more quickly than anyone else in the race and Vlad must have felt threatened, ... again, oh well, poor guy.

Singing along to 'A kiss from a rose' by Seal, with ten miles left of this section, I felt the ground start to quiver and heard the growl of an American V8 big-ass truck as it came crawling up next to me. The door flung open, and the most stereotypical Canadian truck driver broke out in conversation with me, asking the usual question of how I was feeling and did I want some chocolate or a hot coffee. The locals are always so friendly, and they really do love this race. They are astounded that we even want to attempt something so stupid. After a few minutes of chat, he wished me good luck and lit up the big V8 again, shaking the ground I stood on. Returning to Seal, I didn't even have time to get a kiss from a rose before another vehicle came cruising up next to me. This time a 4x4, and as the window came down to a couple with two of the biggest smiles I'd seen, I smelt food, not just food, but hot, greasy, BBQ food. His big booming voice surprised me as he said he had to stop because we both had the same name, mentioning how he'd read my name on the back of the sled, and wanted to say hello. He could tell I'd smelt something intoxicating and offered me some food. He opened a carrier bag and parted some tin foil, showing me a mountain of freshly cooked steaks still glistening and greasy. "Here, take one, we have plenty." "Really?", as my eyes widened, and saliva covered my cheeks. "Yeah, sure, go ahead, son", he continued. Gloves off, I grabbed the closest bit of meat and took a crocodile-sized bite out of the corner. Wow, just wow - unbelievable. The juices squirted everywhere, dribbling down my chin and into my buff. This amazingly-generous guy carried on giving me info but I can't remember a single word. None of my other senses were working, just my taste buds. It was wonderful. Still liking my fingers, I said my appreciation and wished them both a fantastic day before I was left alone once again. The scent of the meat in the buff carried me all the way to CP4, where I witnessed Vlad just leaving as I pulled up next to the trailer.

Once I'd consumed a couple of the dry frozen meals and told the crew about my steak, it was time to get back on with the job at hand. “Where's the next CP then?” “Inuvik” came the response. “Inuvik?” I was confused. “Yep, Inuvik!”. “That's seventy miles away!” There was a sign just outside saying ‘seventy miles to Inuvik’. “Correct”, came the reply. “This is the long section to give you a night out”. “A night out! We’d just spent two bloody days stuck outside near the Arctic circle sign”. “Regardless”, he said “Checkpoint 5 is at Inuvik”.

With this information, a decision needed to be made. Should I pitch my tent here on the cold frozen river and then try for the seventy miles all in one go tomorrow, or get twenty or so miles done this evening, take a nap, and finish the remaining fifty in the morning? It was still only 5pm and I felt great, so I left in hot pursuit of Vlad.

Frustrated …. again!

After only a couple of miles the road steepened sharply, taking me straight up a 500-foot escalator. I was dripping with sweat by the time I got to the top, forcing me to briefly stop to change my layering and get comfortable before the darkness came, and the temperature dropped. Within a few minutes I turned a slight corner, and the next forty miles of road stretched out like a white carpet in front of me. I cannot explain how true and flat the road was. I could see for miles. Tall, heavily snow-coated trees lined either side of the 20-metre-wide gantry for what seemed like eternity.

Vlad was a wispy blur a few miles away which gave me a focus point. As dusk approached, it wasn't just the temperature that dropped. The wind returned and it really started howling. A full-on head wind smashing me in the face, turning forward momentum into a battle. I could still see Vlad from the red light on the back of his sled; that was if I could lift my head enough and focus through watering eyes, but I didn't seem to be gaining on him. Every now and then I could also make out some lights in the distance. This was still a highway, and a few times a day a big powerful articulated truck with a couple of trailers on the back would pass. It would thunder past with its horns flaring to say hello. I assumed these lights were a truck coming, so I'd manoeuvre to the side of the road to stay safe. Unfortunately, the side of the road wasn't as used and flat as the centre. The sled would become heavier as it rolled over the deeper snow, or even worse, shuffled around over the clumps of scattered ice as they were thrown to the side from passing vehicles. Basically, staying close to the side was just a short-term fix to evade the dangers of the passing truck, jumping instantly back to the comfort of the smooth, well-trodden centre, once safety was assured. The thing is, this bloody road was that straight and that flat, it took thirty minutes for those lights to pass. I could see that truck coming from twenty miles away, which meant spending too much time getting annoyed with the bumpy side of the road. Adding to this the turbine of wind that was like a jet stream being guided down a funnel of tall trees, and I started to think that I really wished I had stayed at the checkpoint.

It was about 9pm and I'd had enough. I was exhausted. I made the decision to pitch my tent, so pulled the sled over to the side. It needed to be as far over as possible to keep myself safe and away from vehicles. Just as I started to unzip the sled bag, I heard a voice. The wind was howling so strongly that I hadn't even noticed one of our crew vehicles pull up. They were just checking in to see if everything was sound. I nodded and shouted that I'm about to bed down for a few hours until the storm passes. They instantly argued against my decision, saying it was far too dangerous to pitch there, way too close to the road. There wouldn't be a safe place for about 8km. They continued to explain that there would be a dip in the road about 8 km further on where there would be a frozen river that would give me a chance to get away from any passing trucks. Eight kilometres; I guess I can handle that, I thought as I gave them the thumbs up and started moving forward again. Less than two more hours to go, but maybe one and a half if I get a wiggle on. Then I can escape this road and into the dreamworld for a bit.

Back into the emptiness of the night the wind was shouting at me and my head started to play games. Tiredness was setting in and legs moaning. It felt like such a long time since leaving Fort Mcpherson nearly sixteen hours ago, and now fifty-six miles back down the highway. I began drifting. I knew I was drifting because I would occasionally walk into the built-up snowbanks at either side of the road. Then to make things worse, the wind started carrying some snow, which was like needles coming through my thinly-layered buff. It was time for the goggles, but as soon as I placed them over my eyes they froze up. Time after time I would clear them to try again, but within sixty seconds they froze over again. Giving up on that idea, I covered as much skin as I could and drove each step forward to get to that riverbed. This was really starting to get scaringly tough, as I could feel I was beginning to lose this fight. My eyes began to freeze open, and blinking was painful, as very small pieces of ice would stab my eyes lids as they closed. Another source of light grabbed my attention, but my vision was so blurry I couldn't make out if a truck was coming or if it was my imagination. I had hallucinated before when I was here ten years ago when I imagined a family of four in their swimming costumes walking along next to me as if they were on their summer holidays and heading to the pool. This time though, I was sure it was a truck, so I moved to the side just to be sure. It looked as though the light was moving with me and was heading directly into my path, so I moved to the other side of the road, and the bloody light moved with me again. It's got to be a truck, I thought, and the bastard was trying to hit me, unless the driver was drunk. Maybe the driver was asleep and was bouncing off the snow embankments. The light was swerving everywhere. Wherever I went the light followed. Unfortunately, drink driving is very common up here as there is so little policing and it's a very lonely existence. I continued to move from one side to the other, hoping to be out of the way when it passed me. I think fifteen minutes of panicking must have passed whilst I'd been doing these slalom-type manoeuvres up the road before realising, in my blurred and tired vision, the light was coming from my bloody head torch. Outstanding performance Stu, I thought, as I lowered my head in shame.

It was now 1am, and I swear I'd covered about 20 km since the crew had told me the dip in the road was only 8 km further on. I must have missed it, I reflected, and besides, I had absolutely nothing left to give tonight. It was time, and it was safer for me to stop, get comfortable in my sleeping bag and tent, and then take on tomorrow when it comes. I appreciated the concerns directed to me from the crew when they said it was too dangerous to pitch next to the road, so I climbed onto the snowbank to flatten an area. Not the most ideal or comfortable place, but a bit safer. Within a second or so of unravelling my tent, the relentless wind picked it up and sent it rolling down the road. I was in no fit state for a game of chase, but that tent was the only thing that could keep me alive. If it wasn't such a dangerous situation, it would have been almost funny. I jumped onto the tent to prevent it rolling any further down the road, gathered it up and battled with it like a ship's sail back to the sled. This took any last energy I had left. The crying didn't help as I stood next to the snowbank trying to think how I could make this bloody sail my home. Wiping my face, I stepped back from the situation and took a breath. As always, I just need to tick one box at a time. Weigh it down, I thought. I took everything out of the sled and placed it into the unpitched tent. First box ticked. This was enough to hold it in place as I clipped the poles in position and pegged it down. It did take a lot longer than the ninety seconds it had taken when practising in the safety of my garden, but I did have two useless lumps at the end of my arms instead of hands by this stage. Clambering in, I realised in my mentally-dysfunctional state that I had made a huge school-boy error and erected the tent with the opening facing the blizzard. This created a mini-Narnia screen inside the tent. Everything was white from the floor to the ceiling; all my bags, sleeping mat and sleeping bag were covered. Dusting them off and clearing out as much of the snow as I could in my shivering state, I slid into the bag.

Once again, I had left some sugary treats in the sleeping bag to lift me, and I managed to drink some hot water as well. I was warming up, and for a few moments believed I'd overcome another obstacle. I was starting to feel joyous and surprisingly lucky to be in this position; a position and place in the world that only a handful of people will ever experience. Lying in a tent, on my own, in the arctic, with a blizzard battering the sides, and actually feeling confident I had what it took to weather the storm, as it were. This didn't last long though. Within minutes, my body heat melted all the remaining snow inside my humble home and soaked everything, including my sleeping bag. Down-filled sleeping bags and water don't mix. The bag became useless, and my uncontrollable shivering returned. Trying to figure out how I was going to tick this box, I remembered what I promised Teri. Don't do anything stupid and get permanently hurt. The sleeping bag was the only thing I had to get me safely through the night, and there wasn't a hope in hell of drying it out. Unable to think of the next box to tick, and whilst hysterically panicking, partly because I was emotionally and physically spent and partly because I knew I had failed again, I reached for the panic button to get help.

It wasn't long before I was being dragged from the tent and thrown into the back of a 4x4 with my belongings. Arriving in Inuvik an hour later, and after being assisted into a chalet, I sat underneath the warm covers on a comfortable bed crying into my hot food. I didn't want or deserve this comfort. I'd been beaten once again. The guilt and remorse were overwhelming, and I spent the whole night trying to understand what had happened the previous night, and what I could have done differently. Thinking about Teri, Myia and Keira, and how many times I would let them down. It was a long, lonely night, although I did manage to contact Teri to explain what happened and to let her know I was safe, but I'm pretty sure nothing that came out made sense.

Noticing a little movement outside the chalet in the morning, I cleaned myself up and headed off to HQ to ask how everyone else, still in the race, was doing. I was told there were nine left. "Natalie and Tom are still storming ahead and could probably finish tomorrow, which would beat the overall record for the race by over a day", the crew member said. "Wow, that's astonishing", I replied. This had stood for thirteen years and was set by ultra-running royalty Mimi Anderson. "Then came Vlad who had just left CP5 and was on his way to Inuvik. Then there's"…"Hold on, hold on a minute", I interrupted. "Checkpoint 5 is Inuvik, and how did Vlad get to Inuvik so quickly? No way did he do seventy miles through the night". "Inuvik is checkpoint 6" the crew replied, "Caribou Creek is checkpoint 5." "What the…. where the fuck is Caribou Creek? When did that come into the game plan?", "It's about 30 miles outside of Inuvik," they responded, without even looking up. "You're telling me, there was a checkpoint halfway along that fucking road?", and it turned out I was only about eight miles from it. "What the actual fuck?", I was fuming. "I wouldn't have even left checkpoint 4 if I'd known there was a checkpoint just over forty miles away. I only went out because I had been told it was supposed to be a 70+ mile section of the race. What the fuck?", I repeated. "I shouldn't have even been out in that fucking storm; I would still be in the bloody race," I grunted, as I stormed out to find Martin, who as per usual couldn't be found.'

From my understanding of the events, it was only Vlad and myself who received the wrong information. After I left checkpoint 4 an hour or so behind Vlad, word came through the grapevine that another checkpoint was going to open at Caribou Creek to split the long section up. Everyone behind me received this new direction and slept at the 4th checkpoint, missing the storm. The two leaders out the front weren't affected because they had covered that much distance when we were stuck at the Arctic circle; they were shipped nearly twenty miles past CP4 when we restarted. It was just Vlad and myself that, in my opinion, got screwed. Vlad didn't make it to Inuvik. He was pulled shortly after checkpoint 5 because of damage he received whilst being stuck out in the storm with me. He stumbled past Caribou Creek checkpoint without knowing it was there, and he was surprisingly dragged in, equally as pissed with the situation as I was. The day after, he was evicted from the race because of his threatening and aggressive behaviour towards Martin and was escorted to the airport and out of Canada by the Police. It was a total shit show and cost both Vlad and myself a finish I feel we had both earned and deserved.

I decided to get home as quickly as I could. I didn't want to be around the race, the Arctic or even Canada. I was emotionally wrecked, constantly switching from anger, grief, frustration and guilt. There was a flight out of Inuvik the next day which would take me to Whitehorse. I could then collect the rest of my possessions, which I had left in the hotel, before jumping on the return flights back to the UK.

With one more night left in Canada, I opted to join some of the others for some food and a night out in Inuvik. The last time I was here I remembered the town had a few drinking holes, a couple of restaurants and even a nightclub. This is where they would have the odd bit of local music, but this time it was a different story. Unfortunately, Covid hadn't been too kind and had pretty much destroyed business life in this town.

The population was significantly decreased with just a hardy few, mostly drunk, scattered about. Most places were now boarded up, leaving the only place left to grab a drink, and the possibility of something to eat, was the old nightclub. Entering the venue, the six of us doubled the population of the bar. It hadn't changed a jot in the last ten years, apart from a big sign behind the bar saying CASH ONLY. As none of us were carrying any cash, we were pointed towards a free-standing cash machine in the middle of the hallway which charged a fortune to make a withdrawal. Grabbing a pint, we asked if there was any food locally. "Aarrr, yes my friend", was the reply, "we do food," and with that he pulled out the menu from behind the bar. This was a torn-off piece of card from a cardboard box with the selection of meals written on it in felt tip pen. Each option on the menu was a different colour and written in capital letters. We were instructed to make our selections and call the number at the bottom of the cardboard. Keeping the smirks and chuckles to a minimum, we made our selections. The choices were fish fingers and chips, sausage and chips, beef burger and chips, or egg and chips. We all nervously made our selections based on what would be the safest to eat and rang the number, but no answer, someone else tried the number. No answer. Calling the bartender over, we explained nobody was answering. With a firm swipe he grabbed the piece of cardboard and went behind the bar to call the number himself. No answer. Now slightly miffed, he marched from behind the bar, past us, and opened a door on the other side of the room shouting through it in a strong, rough and slurred Canadian, accent "Will ya answer the bloody phone!". He then disappeared into the kitchen, making all the pans clatter to show his frustration, before storming back out, past us once again, and climbing the stairs through another door. We heard him heavy-footed cross the hallway above our heads and slam opens a doorway before shouting at someone, “We av fuckin customers ya lazy bastard. Get your drunken ass downstairs”. Then it went quiet for a few seconds before we heard a bit of a tussle, a few more strong words exchanged, and another heavy-footed retreat. On re-entering the bar, and sweeping his hair back under his baseball cap, the bartender came up to us and apologised in the poshest voice he could muster, “I’m sorry, but I’m afraid the kitchen is closed this evening”. He then shuffled off behind the bar again, leaving a stench of cannabis behind him. It was just brilliant. I would have paid for that entertainment anywhere else. It was just perfect, and even cheered me up a bit, if just for a few minutes.

Leaving the club, we were luckily directed by a local to a pizza place that was around the corner; so our bellies did eventually get filled, and by something, I’m guessing, a lot safer than what would perhaps have come out of that kitchen!

Arriving back at the chalet close to midnight, Canada did give me one last treat before I left. The Aurora Borealis began darting around the sky. It was a truly amazing spectacle, especially in such a dark sky, and no picture will ever be able to capture its wonder. That night was the coldest I've ever experienced; somewhere around minus 45 degrees Celsius, but we didn’t care. The exposed skin felt instantly painful and damaged, giving us only a short window to admire this surreal magical dance.

The rest of the journey home was a tough one. Definitely the toughest yet. I had no idea how I was going to be able to lift myself up from this fall. I was already mentally falling whilst on the plane and couldn't see a light at the end of it. Explaining this was going to be equally as tough as exiting the race itself. I needed to find a way to dig deep, I needed something I could rely on, something that would enable me to pull myself back up from the floor.

Chapter 5

Five Pillars

The rest of 2023 was tough. It wasn't just the incompleteness and withdrawal from the race that made the year uncomfortable; it was just a rough year. The unpleasantness of the race left a few scares. I really didn't know how to start rebuilding from it, and even now I am still pretty pissed off about the whole experience. Mainly, and this is just my opinion once again, about the incompetence of the organisers. That was the 14th edition of the race, and I can't believe that in such a harsh unpredictable environment they haven't got back-up plans. I mean, that's all they preach about when educating and warning the athletes about preparing for such a challenge. Be prepared for everything! Think on your feet! Have a plan for any scenario! That, along with the fact I didn't even get an apology. That race cost me thousands of pounds and thousands of hours of blood, sweat and tears in preparation.

I was a bit lost and felt rather flat for the whole year. Everything was done at a 'just good enough', or 'that'll do' pace, just enough to get through another day. No connection was made to anything, and everything was a six out of ten, just so I could tick it and say I'd done it. I didn't really race for the rest of the year. Well, I did take part in another 24-hour endurance race called the Equinox 24, but that was only because I had around twenty of the gym members also running. I didn't feel it though and pulled out after six hours to support everyone else, sort of. But in reality, I spent most of the remaining eighteen hours drifting in and out of sleep in my tent. My exercise didn't have any focus at all. I ran a little, rowed a little, lifted a couple of weights, walked quite a bit, but nothing with any direction or conviction. I was broken and needed to find a way to start again from the foundations up.

It was, however, a big year for us as a family. It was my 50th birthday, along with two big birthdays for my daughters who turned 21 and 18. We decided to have an all-out, one last big family holiday treat and went to New York. I don't know if you've ever been to New York, but it's nuts. Everything you have ever seen in movies about NYC is totally true. There is no place like it, nobody cares what you are doing or wearing; anything goes. There are yellow cabs everywhere, people off their heads on crack and arguing with the wall they are standing in front of or having full-on two way discussions with themselves as they walk past. People asleep on the floor in cardboard boxes right next to a Rolls Royce or a Ferrari. The place is just so high. The city touches the sky, and once you step foot into Central Park the noise really does just disappear. The noise on the streets is unrelenting. At any time of the day or night you can hear car horns, people shouting and emergency service sirens. And steam; steam really does come out of every manhole cover, just like in the movies. Where's it come from? I began to accept how bonkers New York was when I was standing on a crossroads with my family in Times Square late in the evening, waiting for the green light so we could cross. Looking to the left of me was a guy dressed in a suit that probably cost more than my car, holding a suitcase and talking on his phone about finance, I think; and to the right three women dressed in tutus around their waist and a little piece of coloured tape covering their nipples; that was it. They were chatting away about their kids' week at school as if their appearance was normal. Over the road, Mario from Mario Kart was talking to Batman. On the other corner was Spiderman hanging from a streetlight with a couple of photographers snapping away at him, next to two cops on horseback talking to some Disney princesses. There was also some guy standing in the middle of the junction dressed to the nines with a purple fur coat that flowed behind for a good two metres, also being snapped at by a couple of photographers. I'm guessing he was one of these so-called influencers. All this was going on and nobody gave a shit. The other thousand people just continued on in their own worlds. So surreal.

This New York trip was also a defining moment because we left for this family bucket-list trip the day after I permanently locked the doors of the gym. We had been struggling for a couple of years, ever since the Covid lockdowns. The pandemic eventually beat us and we had no money left to support the company. It was doomed from the beginning. We had opened our doors eight weeks before we first heard the words 'Covid 19' and pandemic, then spent four and a half years trying to hold on, but it wasn't to be. I think the leisure industry, especially gyms, were some of the worst hit by the pandemic with over 25% of all gyms and studios closing. That works out to 1.5 million people in the health and fitness industry losing their jobs. I sold what I could, paid off what I could, and with what was left and some help from my Health Coaching clients, managed to scrape enough funding to build a studio in my garden, which is where I am now. I've gone full circle and returned to doing what I do best, which is working with people on a 1-2-1 basis. This does have its positives and negatives. It's a lot easier, more time for myself and my family, and there are less expenses, but for the first few months I did feel very claustrophobic and became agoraphobic. Over the three months after our return from New York, I only went from the house to the garden, with an occasional visit to the supermarket. Not very healthy for a wandering mind like mine.

It was in the March, six months before New York that we felt something switch, and realised the business was definitely going to fall. March really hit us hard, as everyone seemed to stop spending. Membership in the gym halved in three weeks. My wife's pet caring business went down by 70% in the same period, and worryingly, we started struggling financially. Month on month our income was being subsidised by the little pension we had. The help I had hired in the gym to relieve me for a few hours had to be stopped, so I was working over seventy hours a week and still losing money. Things were really starting to affect all of us. I could feel the weight bearing down on all our shoulders during the six months of torture it took before eventually switching the lights off and giving back the keys. Six months of minimal communication between us, counting the pennies again, and not knowing what to do next. We all seemed to take it in turns to be ill. Just low-level issues; colds, flus, stomach bugs, skin conditions, and so on. Just stuff that would make life difficult, but not bad enough to stop us and force a recovery period in bed. We were all slightly on edge and arguments about nothing were creeping in.

After one particular disagreement in June, when we were all in separate rooms and slowly trying to calm down, I was in the living room staring at the wallpaper trying to understand how to get control of this situation. This was, I believe, the moment I made the decision to say, 'Fuck it' and close down the gym, but I didn't want to make that decision whilst angry, disconnected, tired and dysfunctional. I needed to be in control of what I could be in control of. I needed to get myself and us back on top and move forward with whatever we could. When you feel you're on a downward spiral and things are out of your control, you feel shit and life just won't stop kicking you. You have to try to step away, step back, force something to change that is in your control, no matter how small. This could be the thing that could start the spiral heading up instead of down. We needed a lift, we needed something to, firstly, give us the emotional strength to make closing the gym a reality, and a positive reality at that. Secondly, having control of something, anything, when everything around us seemed to be out of control. And lastly, to remind us that the business and our finances weren't the most important thing. We are! Our health, our relationships and our happiness. Business is just business, and money is just money. It will come and go. Whether you currently have some or not shouldn't change your health, your relationships with your loved ones, or your happiness. These are all things that money shouldn't dictate.

I remembered something I used to preach to the girls when they weren't feeling right or weren't in control. If they had a headache, a spot, or a cold, or felt emotionally down or out of control; if they were tired or frustrated; If they didn't know which direction to take or just generally felt wrong or broken, I would tell them it was time to assess their five pillars. Look at your pillars. Do any of them need rebuilding, repairing or strengthening? Look at your fundamentals, I would say, and they knew what I was referring to, even if it was with a roll of the eyes. The five pillars are something I made up a few years ago. They are the foundations of your house, the house you live in every day of your existence. Basically you, your physical, physiological and spiritual presence, all added together, i.e. your house. The foundations that hold you all together and keep you standing up are your five pillars. If they are strong, they'll help you to be happy, productive, healthy and loving.

If there is something that needs repairing in your life, look at your five pillars and ask yourself honestly, have you been looking after them? If not, you need to rebuild and repair the cracks first, before contemplating anything else. No house will stand for long without strong foundations. Once the pillars are strong, you will feel back in control and everything else will just seem to fall back into place.

My five pillars.

Ask yourself: -

1. Have you eaten nutritionally?
2. Have you kept hydrated?
3. Have you had sufficient sleep?
4. Have you exercised daily?
5. Have you breathed in fresh air daily?

Simple, you would think, but I guarantee that, If you are below par, then one of these is crumbling, and I would even take a guess that if one is crumbling they are all suffering, and becoming weak, ready to fall.

If you are eating convenient, sugary, processed foods, I would put money on you not hydrating properly, and sleep is probably being affected as well. Exercise is the last thing on your mind, and if someone suggested going out for a walk just for the sake of walking, this would probably ignite a verbally-aggressive response.

Becoming dehydrated affects sleep patterns and reduces the processing of nutrients in your food, even if you are eating healthily. It causes depression and anxiety, reducing the desire to exercise or even take a break to absorb a bit of nature.

Cutting corners with your quality and quantity of sleep is the easiest way to create an extra thirty minutes of so-called functional time, but reduces the quality of your cognitive functioning, focus, drive, and ability to make decisions.

Exercise is the most underrated necessity in the modern world. The hormonal reaction from exercise makes everything - all the other pillars, not just easier to maintain, but you'll feel driven to make them stronger.

Pillar number five is fresh air. Underestimate the power of breathing and fresh air and you'll spend your whole life trying to understand why you continually think something is missing. Out in the open, away from straight lines, is where you manifest change. This is where you make the decision to build and strengthen your pillars. We are supposed to be outside. We feel free outside. This is where all the answers are.

I'm assuming you already know that eating healthily, drinking water, exercising, maintaining a good sleep pattern and grabbing some fresh air, are all beneficial to your mental and physical well-being. If you don't, we have some deeper issues to correct first. So why don't you do it? Why don't I always do it? Why is it so hard to look after five simple pillars; five fundamental habits that hold up the rest of your life?

Life is hard, and the demands that are forced upon us by others, and ourselves, raises the expectations we think we deserve from life. These expectations become our priority and not ourselves, and as much as we know we should work on our pillars, we tell ourselves we haven't got time.

Where am I supposed to fit in time to take a walk? I haven't got the time or money to join a gym! I get fifteen minutes a day to prepare a meal for the family before getting back to work! - Sleep, I wish - between looking after a family, a job, a house, cleaning, cooking, washing, etc., etc. I am lucky if I get five hours. I know I'm supposed to drink more water, but with everything going around in my head, I forget.

The ironic thing is that, if you focused on the fundamentals first, you would become more focused, dependable, balanced, energetic and productive. Everything you struggle with would become easier, creating more time for yourself and others. You'd have time to be a parent instead of a dictator; you'll have more energy for your partner and want to reconnect with mates you feel guilty about ignoring. Your life-juggling skills will develop because of the new power you feel from, one, being in control and, two, being better at everything you're doing.

I'm assuming you do know what the path looks like. But do you know what a strong pillar looks like? Do you understand the benefits each pillar brings to the house? Let's go over the five pillars in a little more detail so you have the knowledge to repair them if there are cracks. Then you only have to make the choice of whether to walk the path or not, because knowing it and walking it are two totally different things.

Nutrition

There is so much information out there in the cyber world, in gyms, on adverts, as well as from acquaintances and friends. Basically, every time you lift your head someone is trying to advise you about a diet or a fad or a miracle tablet, something that will make you feel healthier, lose weight, build muscle or make you live longer. The biggest and most profitable area in health and fitness is the diet and supplement industry. Slimming World had a revenue of £921 million last year, Weight Watchers £530 million. Slimfast sold £212 million worth of shakes, and Herbalife reported sales of $5.1 billion. The whole of the supplement industry worldwide is estimated to be worth $400 billion dollars or £300 billion pounds, and the health and fitness industry, in all its shapes and forms, is worth $5.6 trillion dollars. I don't even know what that figure means; what is a trillion? With that much money being spent on supplements alone, as we try to stay healthy and fit, you would think we would all be like athletes, but no! Why is it we are in the middle of an obesity and diabetes pandemic that's casting a shadow over the covid one. Sadly, it has been estimated that seven million people have died from Covid so far, and in a high percentage of these cases the patient had pre-existing illnesses. Obesity alone has drastically killed seventy million people since the turn of the century, and each year the figure increases. Why isn't this pandemic all over the news, why aren't we being helped and instead we're being guided towards all the diet plans and supplements? £450 billion pounds of revenue, taxable revenue. That's why.

It doesn't matter if you are watching the latest documentary or listening to an influencer on Tiktok, every single one is guiding you to buy a product; every documentary is funded by a company that wants to show a particular result that makes you live and spend a certain way. It's all about the money. The whole industry is corrupt, misguided and strangely, not influenced by the need to improve people's health.

Food and diet shouldn't be complicated. We have managed for hundreds of thousands of years without the need for supplements and calorie restrictive diets, which, when it comes down to it, is all the diet industries are doing. In their own way, they are cleverly putting you on a calorie restrictive diet. Whether it's counting points, sins, traffic-lighted foods, drinking shakes or cutting out meals, it's all about calorie restriction. This just doesn't work. Our hunger hormones don't behave well when we spend time consuming less calories than we even need to maintain our RMR (resting metabolic rate). This is the number of calories we use each day just to stay alive. Our physical mass, but mainly muscle mass, requires a certain number of calories to stay alive. Even if we don't move, lie on the floor and stare at the ceiling for twenty-four hours, we still burn calories. My RMR is roughly 2,000 calories a day. If I spend too many days consuming less than that, my hormones panic as my weight drops. Not just my fat weight, but my muscle weight, resulting in less muscle mass and a lower RMR. If I was to lose five kilos of muscle, that would reduce my RMR by roughly seventy-five calories per day. Therefore, making it a lot easier to regain the weight when I go back to normal calorie consumption, and encouraging a yo-yoing effect regarding my weight, as I will need to go back to a weight-loss programme. This is how so much money can be made in this industry, as the manufacturers rely on this yo-yo dieting that supports customer retention.

Spending too much time below your RMR triggers the hunger hormones leptin and ghrelin to work together to regain the weight you lost, and maybe a little more, just in case you return to an environment where food could be scarce again. After all, the job of your hormones is to keep you alive in the environment you live in. If you go through a period of extreme weight loss, they panic and fix the issue as soon as they can. The best way to lose weight is slowly, maintaining your RMR calorie intake and exercising your excess weight away. It might take longer, but it will stay off.

Be careful where your calories come from. All the food and drink we consume is categorised into three macronutrients: carbohydrates, proteins and fats. Carbohydrates, or carbs, are the main energy supply; proteins, are the builders and maintenance crew, and fats help you with nutrients and vitamins, and do a vital job of keeping your organs warm. Think of it like this; Imagine you are building a house. To build this house successfully and strongly you need three things: the materials, the work force and the knowledge of how to put it all together. Carbs are your workforce. Without them you will know what you are doing and have the materials, but no one to put it all together. The protein is the bricks, wood, cement and slate. Without it you have the crew to do the job, and you have the instructions to put it all together, but the suppliers haven't turned up. Fat: Well, that's your know-how. Fat has the answers and keeps everything moving and ticking over nicely. Without fat you have a field full of the bits and pieces, like a scattered jigsaw of a house, and a bunch of grafters lying around in the sun getting paid for nothing because nobody knows what to do.

Cut any one of these macronutrients out and your house will fall. Basically, you are the project manager. It's your job to make sure there is an adequate supply of all the essentials needed for a successful build. Not too much and not too little. So where can you find the three ingredients to make the project run smoothly? Proteins and fats come mainly from the same source which is animals and animal produce, like dairy and eggs. There are other ways of getting proteins and fats, such as nuts, seeds, avocados, beans, legumes, soy, and hemp, but the majority of our diets' protein and fat has come from meat and animal produce throughout our history. Carbohydrates are everything else we eat and drink that cannot be classified as a protein or fat. Every vegetable and fruit; everything beige from bread products to pasta shapes; anything that has any type of grain in it, any alcoholic drink; or fizzy drink, anything that has any form of sugar in the list of ingredients. In fact, pretty much anything that has an ingredients list on the packaging and has been ready made, has some form of carbohydrate in it. Carbohydrate is a posh word for sugar. Bread is sugar, pasta is sugar, rice is sugar, crisps are sugar, broccoli is sugar, oranges are sugar, carrots are sugar, beer is sugar, gin is sugar, and all food and drink that is not a protein or a fat is sugar. Sugar is our energy, and if we consume more sugar than we burn, we will store it for another day.

We are programmed through hundreds of thousands of years of living in the wild like bears to store sugar as fat for when winter comes. Our circadian rhythm has developed from experiencing summers, when there is an abundance of food available, and winters when all the small animals are hibernating, there's no more fruit on the trees and the root vegetables have stopped growing. This has established, in its own natural way, a yo-yo diet routine. We are programmed genetically to gain weight straight after a weight loss. We yo-yo from winter to summer, to winter, to summer. Only now we don't have to worry about winter because of supermarkets. We can get fifty thousand calories delivered to our door with a click of the button any day of the year. It's constantly summer. Regrettably our hormones have not adapted to this new life and continue to store carbohydrates for the forthcoming winter that never arrives; until, that is, you go on a weight-loss regime.

There are two different types of carbs, or sugars if you want to call them that: Simple carbs or complex carbs. Simple carbs are generally carbs that have no fibre in them, which is typically anything that has sugar and processed grains in it. The biggest culprit is wheat. When we take wheat and turn it into all the wonderful shapes we love to eat, such as bread, bagels, wraps, scones, cakes, croissants, pasta, spaghetti, lasagna, and most ready-made meals, the fibre has been greatly reduced, making it a quick carb, and the biggest problem with simple carbs is the lack of fibre. In complex carbs, the fibre is what makes it complex. The fibre makes the food harder to break down, which slows the release of energy from the food into the blood, or I should say the release of sugar into the blood. This creates a reduced insulin response compared to the same calories eaten from a simple carb. This reduced need for an insulin response will lower the possibility of diabetes, high cholesterol, high blood pressure and heart disease, along with a whole host of other issues, from joint problems to neurological problems, as well as some cancers. Without fibre to slow down the digestion process, a 200-calorie four-fingered Kit Kat would take only a minute to be absorbed into the blood, creating a massive sugar spike and a massive insulin release. This insulin comes from your pancreas, and the pancreas can only make so much before it starts running dry or wearing out, much like a car engine. It doesn't matter how well you look after it, it will eventually die, and your car will be ready for the graveyard. Every time you demand a big insulin response by eating a simple carb, you are pressing the accelerator of the car to the floor and red lining the engine, or pancreas. This reduces its life expectancy and brings on a breakdown, or diabetes. Whereas, eating two hundred calories of vegetables, which would be the equivalent of eating a whole broccoli, a whole cauliflower, a leek and a courgette all at the same time, would be a very slow absorption of the sugar, because of the fibre. This slower drip, drip, drip of sugar into the system wouldn't panic the pancreas at all. It's more than likely that the energy dripping into the bloodstream would be used up at the same rate by just proceeding through your normal daily living activities and probably preventing an insulin response altogether. It would save those unspent miles for another day, reducing the onset of diabetes, and minimising storage for the winter. The other massive benefit from eating complex carbs over simple carbs is the number of vitamins and minerals in complex carbs, they are fully loaded with everything you need for a healthy life, whereas simple carbs are pretty much just energy-filled cardboard. I'm not saying simple carbs don't have their place, but you need to look at your lifestyle and evaluate whether you need them. Someone who grafts all day, like a builder, a landscaper, or a mechanic, and so on, would burn a lot of energy to get through their day. If they just lived on the calories from complex carbs, they would have to be continually eating because of their low and slow energy release. Without a few mouthfuls of some simple carbs once in a while they might start struggling for energy, but this should not be at the sacrifice of eating complex carbs because of their valuable nutrients and vitamins. But the office worker or taxi driver, someone who sits down most of the day to work, might very quickly gain weight if they include a lot of simple carbs into their diet. They simply do not require the calories from the cardboard.

The number one lesson I give people when they ask for 'one easy-to-follow rule' that helps with weight loss or preventing overeating issues is, 'earn your food before you consume it'. Don't eat it and then expect to be able to burn it away afterwards. Our biology isn't designed to devour a plate full of calories before it has created a void, a space that needs replenishing. Create the demand before satisfying it.

When we wake up after a sleep, our system has been totally replenished and ready for a day of action. An average adult-size human form will hold roughly 1,500 calories of energy in their muscles, and maybe 250 in their liver as a backup. This is so we have the energy to go hunting and gathering or even have to run away from a predator. We spent a lot of our ancestral past without fridges and kitchens. We didn't have much, if any, stored calories to wake up to. We had to use energy to collect energy. The problem now is that we don't go hunting and gathering when we get up; we go downstairs, open the fridge and cupboards to grab a simple carb-loaded breakfast full of wheat and sugar, and proceed to stuff it down our necks before we've even contemplated what the day holds for us. These 500 calories of unnecessary and useless energy consumed during breakfast has nowhere to go. All the muscles and liver cells that can hold them are already still full from sleepy time. Therefore, the only place to store these excess calories, in order to keep your blood sugars balanced, is in your fat cells for when winter comes. Remember though, we can only use the stored winter supply when it's actually winter and there is a shortage of food. So that unnecessary breakfast will give you a short-term sugar rush until your insulin can sort it out and store it away for later. When you haven't eaten for six to eight hours you start going into ketosis. Ketosis is when you run out of the energy you have just eaten and require a different energy source to keep all the systems working. This is when your pancreas reduces the amount of insulin released and starts releasing glucagon instead. Glucagon is the hormone that helps to break down your fat molecules into small-chain fat molecules called ketones. Ketones are then small enough to be directed into the muscle cells, etc., to be used as the alternate fuel supply. This is when you are classed as being a fat burner and not a sugar burner. Think of sugar as petrol and fat as diesel, because they both have the same characteristics. Sugar behaves like petrol, and fat, much like diesel. Petrol is a bit more exciting as it burns more powerfully and easily, but the miles per gallon is less and the life expectancy of the engine is lower. Diesel takes a bit longer to get started, but when it's warmed up, it will run with more consistency and at slower demand for fuel, giving it a longer life expectancy, and you'll get further on a full tank before it runs out.

Spending the start of our day in ketosis is, in my opinion, the healthiest way to control our fuel supply. For thousands of years, we spent the first half of the day gathering the fuel before we would sit down to eat and restock the system for tomorrow's hunt. This is why

I believe that intermittent fasting is the perfect way of controlling our body composition, and to be in sync with our daily hormonal cycle. This is why, more often than not, I don't eat until around midday. I give myself a chance to burn away some of the stored energy in my muscles before eating to replace it, preventing fat storage. The other benefit of not putting food into my guts to process for a longer period of the day, is that digestion is the most demanding 'internal system' we have for our energy. Roughly 20-25% of all energy consumed is used digesting the food we've just eaten. So, whilst our digestion system is churning away, breaking down and processing food, and then deciding what to do with it, other systems are not given enough energy to do their jobs efficiently. For example, our repair and maintenance system and the detox system. If the repair and maintenance system only receives 80% of the required energy it needs that day, then only 80% of the work will get done and you'll age that little bit quicker. If the detox system only gets 80%, then equally only 80% of the toxins that have built up through the day - by eating rubbish, drinking alcohol and coffee, exercising, breathing in fumes, absorbing chemicals through the skin through transdermal absorption and stress - then the other 20% will slowly build up each day. This will eventually need a release and will come out as a cold, flu or a chest infection, or maybe spots or a skin rash. These are the low-level health issues that are a whisper from your body telling you that you're not doing it right. You're not living correctly; something needs to change! Ignore these and the words will continue to come but with a bit more authority behind them. This could be diabetes, high cholesterol and blood pressure, maybe joint problems, or pre-cancerous cells. These issues mean you are receiving a hard kick up the arse, and a world of hurt could be on its way. Ignore these and pass them by as just signs of getting old, then your body will basically say 'Fuck it', I've been telling you for years you haven't been doing it right. You didn't listen to the whispers or the stern talking to, so here, have a heart attack, have a stroke, here's cancer, it's time to put a premature end to this crap. Listen to the whispers before the shouting starts.

I'm not saying intermittent fasting will stop all of the stuff that will hurt you or kill you prematurely, but I am saying it gives you a stronger army with which to fight them away for a longer period. Just give yourself a fighting chance.

So, let's sum it up:

- Stick to the foods that nature provides, i.e. fruit, vegetables, meat, fish, nuts seeds and eggs, and stay away from foods that have an ingredients list. If it has an ingredients list, business has made it; and trust me, business has only made it to make money, not to make you healthy.
- Don't follow any fads or quick fixes because they are all designed to get fast results, but the loss will only be short-lived, because every calorie-restrictive diet will have a negative effect on your hormones, resulting in eventual weight gain.
- Eat a good balance of macronutrients, proteins, fats and carbohydrates, but stay away from the simple carbs, because if they are not used up they will be stored for a winter that never comes.
- Burn the calories before you replenish them, because trying to eat energy before you've

burnt it will only result in weight gain and permanent hunger as you constantly try to keep the petrol engine burning.

- Spend some time each day extending your ketosis. Give your body a chance to repair and detox more efficiently for a longer period of time. Stay younger and free from illness for as long as possible. You can't reverse ageing; you can only slow it down.
- Lastly, eat as much organically-produced food as possible, and eat locally-supplied produce where possible; from your local farmer, butcher, and market. Not just because the products are usually better cared for, instead of quickly and cheaply grown or raised in large quantities, but to support local business and reduce your carbon footprint.

Hydration

Many of my stories I push onto my clients in my club, started out years ago in my daughters' bedrooms. I tried to find a way a ten-year-old could understand and relate to a particular lesson. So, I apologise if it sounds as if I'm talking to a ten-year-old, because I was when I made up this story about why we should drink more water.

Imagine you have just turned eighteen years old and have become an adult. You are allowed to live in your own home which you quickly buy within a few days. You now have your own pride and joy; you feel on top of the world, and you are the master of your own destiny. You start by making up all your own house rules, because you now understand why I nagged you all those years to respect and look after my house. You understand how horrible it is when your house is out of order. This new little world of yours is amazing, everything you've ever dreamed of. It has all the modern conveniences, and a feel of freshness, excitement, comfort and cleanliness. The perfect place to begin an adventurous life. You walk into your new life a few days after your 18th birthday with a smile that would tame a wild beast and goosebumps the size of the French alps, with a softly-sighed promise to yourself that you will treasure this foundation of your life, knowing that this will make every other adventure possible, and a place you can always come back to when things don't go quite as planned.

As the sun rises and pierces through the curtains on the first morning in your newly acquired home it's 7am and all is at peace with the world. That is, until there is a sudden rattle at the front door, a rattle that shakes the boards and agitates the birds whistling in the trees outside the window, forcing them to fly away. As you make your way down the stairs, you hear the murmurings of many voices chit-chatting outside the front door with a faint musical beat behind it. With anticipation, you pull open the door to reveal fifty of your wide-eyed and excited friends staring at you. For a fraction of a second there's silence before the hustle and bustle of a house-warming party erupts in your new home. A crowd of 18-year-olds with the intent of having the time of their lives. There are drinks of all shapes, sizes and colours, cigarettes and maybe something stronger, pizza everywhere, music blaring from all directions, lights flashing, dancing, and many other antics you can imagine coming from a party with fifty teenagers.

The day lives up to all expectations, proving to be one for the memory banks, lasting until 11 o'clock that evening when the last of the guests wobble reluctantly out the door and down the driveway. Closing the door behind them and turning around to witness the damage in your new home, your jaw drops. Total destruction. Empty beer cans, bottles of wines and spirits everywhere, some of them used as ashtrays, half-eaten pizza dropped in a corner and regurgitated pizza in the opposite corner, underwear circling the room because they are attached to the ceiling fan, furniture forced on its end to make room for the frolicking, and a smell that would need a bit more than a little plug-in to take away. Basically, your home now looks like it's on the brink of death. It looks like the remnants of the parties you wish you had been invited to. There was only one thing for it; time to get the mop, and all the other cleaning equipment out. This can't wait until morning; it has to be done immediately. So, with that you spend the next few hours scrubbing, scraping, polishing, mopping, vacuuming and ventilating the whole house until there's not a hint of evidence left from the party, apart from two bulging black disposable bin bags. You place these on the street outside your home ready for the waste disposal people to collect before morning breaks once again.

Day two arrives in your new home and it turns out to be such a perfect morning once again. Eyes slowly widen, ears absorb the twittering of the birds outside the window, your heart starts beating a little quicker, and your breathing accelerates in anticipation of another exciting day. Muscles start twitching and the neurological connections in the grey matter start to categorise and prioritise your day's activities. Then, suddenly, a clatter from the front door knocker again. Just like yesterday it happens to be 7 o'clock in the morning, and with a glance out the bedroom window you notice fifty of your friends shouting up at you to open the front door. They are looking for a repeat performance of yesterday's hilarities. Not wanting to let them down, you throw on your party outfit and proceed to join them in another frolic around your home, as they destroy everything in their wake, again. Evening time arrives, and around 11pm you manage to force the last drunken bum out of your house and into a taxi. Just as the previous evening, all the shit left behind needs cleaning up before sleepy time. So, with a mop in hand, cloth over your shoulder and polish attached to your waist, you do the necessary duties of scrubbing every bit of evidence of the party away before placing the two bulging black bags of rubbish outside for the waste disposal people to collect before the break of dawn.

It's now the morning of day three and you can't believe it. As regular as clockwork, the whole process starts again with the same fifty friends, in the same way. At the crack of dawn, all the way through the day and until sundown, your fifty friends use your house as the local night club, with the same outcome, and the same two bags of empty beer cans, pizza, curry, drugs, cigarettes, dirty underwear and vomit.

This continues all week, then all month and all year. Every single day a party happens in your home, destroying it, leaving it in need of a big clean-up and some repair work. Every day, two black bags are left outside for the waste disposal to collect, take away and leave the street clean and tidy for the next day. This Groundhog Day has become the norm. In fact, you can't remember a time when this wasn't part of your life. You actually develop a level of contentment with the routine; it feels normal and everything flows sweetly, until one day, on the news, you discover the waste disposal team are going on strike for a month. They are refusing to work for a whole month. It might be over working conditions, wages, pensions, or perhaps because the Council refused to get decaf coffee, who knows? The problem with this is that your parties continue, and the two black bags continue to pile up outside your beautiful home. Three weeks into the strike and you have stockpiled forty-two bags of vomit, junk food, dirty underwear. Etc. The street really starts to stink, vermin start to arrive, disease and infections start travelling around the house and infiltrating your lovely neighbourhood. Mopping, vacuuming, polishing and dusting has no response. The area is basically contaminated. You get the picture…the house you acquired on your 18th birthday is starting to fall apart. It's looking old, it smells, there are stains everywhere, and the locals are blaming you for bringing down the area.

Now relate that to the actual house you wake up in every day, the house that is under construction from your embryonic stage to your full development at eighteen years old. The house you have a party in everyday and use for the adventure of your life. YOUR BODY, the most important house you will ever have. The house that needs to carry you through all your ups and downs and will be there when the shit hits the fan, if you look after it.

Every day you wake up, you breathe more deeply. Your heart rate increases, your muscles become alive, your hormones become stimulated, you take in information through all your senses and react to them. You might go to the gym, go out for a meal, have an argument, consume some alcohol or inhale something toxic. You're participating in your own little party. These needs cleaning up and any damage repaired. When you lay your head on the pillow at the end of a hard day and your eyelids touch, the seven dwarfs come out with their mops, dusters, brushes and tool kit, and then spend the next few hours revitalising your beautiful home ready for the next day's party. When all the chores, repairs and cleaning has been done, and the leftovers, damages and toxins remain, it's all put into two black bags and placed out the front to be collected and dispatched. The only thing left to be done is to wait for waste disposal to come past, collect the bags and take them to be disposed of.

The question is, what is the waste disposal? In your body, in your house, what has the job of taking the waste out?

The answer, of course, is water!

Water is the key. Water is the waste disposal. Without sufficient water, you are technically placing your waste disposal on strike. Those bags will build and build, creating smells, disease and infections. Your house will start falling apart and begin showing you that something isn't right with the system. You will start collection points for these bags in other places around the system, other than the healthiest and most efficient place, which is through your waterworks. This is why your first bladder release in the morning is more potent, darker and a bit smelly; it's full of the black bags. If there aren't enough waste disposal teams on duty, the black bags will try to come out of other detox systems, such as your respiratory system, causing colds, chest infections and smelly breath. They might also try to come out through your skin, causing rashes, skin infections and sores. They might even get trapped and end up just hanging around until they build up enough to create bigger issues such as cancers and other diseases.

A simple answer to some of the most regular low-level health issues is to just drink more water. Your brain is 73% water. Does it not stand to reason that, if it's dehydrated, then it cannot control emotions, it cannot solve problems, it cannot multitask and it cannot control your hormones which look after your wellbeing. It's such a simple thing to maintain, and yet it has been estimated that around 75% of the first world is dehydrated. All it takes is three to four pints a day, and you can change your life. A functional waste disposal system, and a healthier mind that can deal with the issues of today's world more productively.

Sleep

I know for a fact that lack of sleep makes the rest of my pillars weak. When I am tired, I have anxiety attacks about mundane problems. My depression pulls me to the dark parts of my psyche very easily, and it's not just me it controls. It creates a shadow that encloses everyone and everything in our home. My food choices, hydration levels, lifestyle habits, and even my exercise become negative and aggressive. I have learned I need at least six hours of sleep a night to keep me pointing in the right direction. Anything less than that, on a regular basis, and I'm starting my daily journey already running uphill. I can handle a day or two of reduced sleep, but as the tiredness builds, I become a ticking time bomb. I very rarely get to enjoy any more than seven and a half hours. On the privileged occasion this happens, I feel as though I'm dragging a chain behind me for the day. My sweet spot is between six and seven hours each night. If I need more sleep, a midday nap is far more beneficial for me, anyway.

I see the ups and downs, physically and emotionally, in people I teach as well as loved ones around me, when sleep is on point or when it's slipping. It's always one of the pillars I ask about first when there's instability in the house, and I can guarantee it's starting to crumble. A good night's sleep seems to be able to cure a lot of issues. I'd often tell people, who seem to be carrying a problem, just grab a glass of water then go and close your eyes for a bit, then we'll talk about whatever it is that's eating you up. Normally, they'll come back with," Don't worry, it'll be ok now". Problem solved.

In the few books I have read about sleep habits, and what happens when you're asleep, it says that, if you could enjoy a totally angelic, perfect life, with no internal or external negative influences or traumas; a life where the air quality was perfect, your diet was organically grown in your own garden, and the meat you eat was loved and treasured; the relationships in your world were perfect, loving, giving and supportive; even down to washing your clothes in the local stream with naturally-made soap and you never used any unnatural products to smell nice, look great or clean with. If this was at all possible; if you were able to live with a halo above your head in a world of perfection, and maintain it through a whole lifetime, you would still need an average of five hours sleep a night. This would be to repair the daily damage that being alive causes to your system.

I don't need you to tell me that this is, of course, totally impossible. Life has moved forward so much that, whether we like it or not, there is extra damage being done every day that needs to be repaired, and most of this maintenance is done whilst we are asleep.

Let's take an average Friday in the life of an office worker in my hometown, - who is married with a couple of kids and maintains a relatively healthy lifestyle. To start with, my hometown sits next to one of the biggest motorways in the UK and is also down the road from the biggest industrial estate in Europe. The air quality here is supposed to be pretty shit, but not as bad as the smog days of the industrial revolution. However, I would, for the sake of this story, say that it takes twenty minutes extra sleep to repair the damage caused by breathing in the air around here. As our case study gets up in the morning, he fuels himself with two cups of coffee and toast, then realises he's late again before noticing he still needs to get fuel on the way to work. This lateness causes a telling-off from his boss. He then spends the rest of the day chasing his tail, trying to get the last things done for the 'end of week' meeting which, as always, has pastries and coffee available. Just scrapping through, he gets out on time and heads to the gym to burn off the week's stress, so he'll be in a good place when he gets home. Returning home, he finds it in a right mess from the kids doing what they do, and an argument follows, when he insists they switch the game console off and tidy up. He then rushes upstairs to get ready for a couple's night out with some friends. Coming home with a belly full of rich food and a liver full of wine he manages to get into bed around midnight.

So, let's look at his day. We'll start with the base of five hours sleep that is the minimum required to repair the day's damage, plus twenty minutes for the air quality. Let's say an hour for a few coffees; another hour for the stress of being late and rushing around all day. Pastries and rich food during the meal might cost him another forty minutes; maybe another hour because of the muscular damage created in the gym; tension from the kids would be another stress of ten minutes, and lastly, the alcohol. This is an hour for each unit of alcohol, that's six hours for the bottle of wine he drank. Quick calculation……. Fifteen hours and ten minutes of sleep required to repair all the damage from the day's activities.

Nobody from the age of three ever usually manages fifteen hours of good quality sleep. I'm lucky if I get anything more than my six and a half hours. So now a decision has to be made. What gets repaired and what doesn't? Imagine you have a triage nurse inside you somewhere, and the nurse's job is to decide what gets worked on and what doesn't. If you were your own triage nurse, and it was up to you where to allocate the sleep time within the body, what would you repair first to make sure you had the best chance of getting through the next day? What would you be prepared to leave until your eyes shut again? The answer is simple, I hope; you would devote the maintenance time on all the things that keep you alive - your heart, liver, kidneys, lungs and brain, etc. Whatever time you had left after repairing the crucial organs, you would spend on everything else, but it wouldn't be long if you only achieved half of the fifteen hours needed. Your skin, hair follicles, muscles, etc, will be ok for another day. We'll sort those out tomorrow night. You did manage to get a solid 7 and a half hours in though, which left seven hours and forty minutes to be passed onto Saturday night's repair schedule. Saturday, yeah right, as if I'm going to get to Saturday night without causing more damage which will need repairing. With a fry up in the morning, an argument, a couple of beers and a takeaway to make up the argument, you need another thirteen hours sleep. Add that onto the leftover hours from the day before.... twenty hours, mmm, that'll work. Just impossible. Those skin cells, hair follicles, eyes and ears will have to wait for another day, then another day, and another. Sadly, this is how we speed up the aging process.

I hope you see where I'm going with this. We never catch up. It's just life, I understand! All I'm saying is, give yourself a chance; grab forty winks in the afternoon on your days off, if you can, and don't give your little builders and maintenance crew so much to repair on a daily basis. You'll be grateful for it, not just the following day, but later in life, and you'll perform so much better in every other part of your world if you don't feel worn out. It only takes about 20-30 minutes to feel refreshed and rejuvenated.

Just one last sobering thought. I read at the end of a book once, that said, for every hour of sleep missed during your life, an hour is reduced at the end. Mmmmmm, that is worth contemplating.

Exercise

I've heard from so many voices and read in so many books that health, fitness, and especially weight loss, is 20% exercise and 80% food. I used to believe that and even taught that. On countless occasions, I would be explaining to clients that they first need to gain some control of their food and then develop an exercise regime. I agree that it's not possible to train out a bad diet, but in recent years I have come to understand that it's a hell of a lot harder to maintain a healthy approach to life without putting exercise first. I have become a firm believer that it all starts with exercise. A nutritional diet, keeping hydrated, achieving a good night's sleep and longing for some fresh air, will never be consistently part of normal life without the hormonal release that exercise provides.

Once exercised, the body craves the nutrients and building blocks needed to repair the cellular damage created from the exercise. Muscles are microscopically torn, lungs have been slightly damaged from heavy breathing, the heart has been forced into being slightly uncomfortable, and the liver and kidneys have worked hard as they try to keep the system clean and productive. All this maintenance and rebuilding requires energy and the right tools to do the job. If fuelled correctly, the workers will make sure that whatever has been damaged through exercise will be repaired stronger, made more productive and with more resilience than before the damage was done. This is to make sure that the next time we have to move to this extremity, we can cope with it more comfortably, giving ourselves a better chance of surviving. These are the basics of body building and improving fitness. Making the heartbeat faster on a regular basis will create micro tears, resulting in the reconstruction of a bigger, stronger heart. Similarly, the hefty breathing encourages a larger lung capacity. The liver and kidneys, along with other organs and systems of the body, get an equally demanding workout, creating adaptations to improve performance. All these repairs and modifications require nutrients, minerals and proteins that are prevalent in natural foods, and you will find it a lot easier to make better food choices when you are hormonally craving them for nutritional purposes.

Exercising obviously heats the body up and moisture is lost through sweat and evaporation. Throwing down a couple of litres of water becomes not just necessary, but easier after exercise. Listen to the body. It very quickly tells you it needs hydrating, and drinking water becomes a habit, just as much as not drinking water is a habit. Exercise will help build the habit of keeping hydrated.

Before the body has done anything physically demanding, the leading emotional hormone surging around your body is cortisol. This is a low-level stress hormone, and it's bigger and stronger partner is adrenaline. Cortisol is the hormone that keeps you on edge, keeps you hyper alert, just in case you are in danger of attack and have to suddenly react. An attack could be emotional, physical or chemical. An emotional attack could be anything that makes you pissed off, angry or worried; being late for work, having an argument or walking through a misty graveyard in the middle of the night. A physical attack could be, running away from something that, in a previous lifetime, wanted to eat you, or it could be you need to fight your prey - in other words, in our modern and very comfortable world, exercise. Chemical attacks could come from sugar, caffeine, alcohol, nicotine or even a more dangerous drug. The combination of all these stresses or attacks, builds the level of cortisol and adrenaline in our blood. High levels of stress hormones will become hazardous to our health over long periods of time. The only safe way to use these hormones is to make them do what they are designed to do, which is to defend and protect us from being harmed or killed. Make them feel they are doing something to help us as they would in the wilds of yesteryear e.g. fight, swim, run, climb, carry, push, pull; basically, natural exercise. Cortisol and adrenaline levels in the blood then drop, promoting a calmer, more content level of being. The five senses we rely on to receive information from the external world, relax for the first time that day because the exercise gave Cortisol a job to do. Our hormones do not understand we now live in a safer world and believe our daily stresses come from a place that could potentially be dangerous. Without daily exercise Cortisol will heighten the senses so we are more prepared for the confrontation of something that might kill us. Sight is sharper, allowing us more time to react to a predatory onslaught. Hearing is not just clearer, but the direction in which the crunch of the leaves comes is more accurate. Touch is heightened as we feel directional changes in the wind, and reaction times become crisper. When down-wind from prey or predator, you can smell precisely what you could be encountering. Also, taste buds wake up with the anticipation of possible food in the not-too-distant future. This is why you crave sugary foods and make bad food choices when you are hormonally living in the cortisol world of low-level stress. Exercise relaxes all the senses, using the cortisol for the exact job it was designed for, and allowing you to make better choices, and become more rational.

Once the stress hormones have been used and the danger has been run away from or fought, the happy and healing hormones can flood the system and do their job. These hormones are called Serotonin, Endorphins, Oxytocin and Dopamine. It's their job to calm you down, to make you feel better about life after the trauma of being attacked, and to repair the damage caused by the forced exercise of running away from, for example, a tiger. It's counterproductive to have the stressful fight and flight hormones in play at the same time as the calming and healing hormones. If this happened, you wouldn't know whether to fight the tiger or cuddle it, so the happy hormones have to sit and wait in the corner until safety is achieved.

Consistent low levels of serotonin can lead to poor memory, low moods, low self-esteem, anxiety, sugar cravings and sleep disturbances. It is a neurotransmitter, meaning it relays information between nerve cells or neurons and also promotes the release of endorphins from the brain and spinal cord. These reduce the feeling of pain, acting as a sedative to reduce the hormonal effects of stress, i.e. cortisol. To increase levels of serotonin, walk in nature and the sunshine, make better food choices, obtain sufficient sleep and make sure you get downtime.

Endorphins are released mainly through exercise, giving you what's known as a runner's high, a similar feeling received from the effects of morphine. Other triggers of endorphins are sex and cocoa, e.g. chocolate, although, because chocolate gives you a quick high, it will also drop you quickly, encouraging a low and therefore emotional attack or stress which will then release cortisol. Not a good choice, really.

Exercise-driven endorphins are one of the biggest armies you have to fight against the effects of cortisol.

Oxytocin makes you feel happy about life. It simply makes you love more and hate less, and it reduces the effects of negativity. Negative environments, negative people, negative habits and negative stimulants; oxytocin reduces the damage done by these. Negativity ages you and is toxic, and it's also very contagious.

Dopamine is released during sex, laughter, satisfaction, pride, achieving something new and learning something new. It can also be released by things like buying new materialistic crap, therapy shopping, affairs, drugs (dope), gambling, and many other quick fixes. Be careful, though, as these can be short-term fixes and often require bigger and more frequent fixes to get the same high. Much healthier to get your dopamine fix from exercising, competing, learning something engaging, having a laugh with loved ones and, of course, having sex with a very much loved one.

So, understanding all this, and although the activity itself has the amazing physical benefits of becoming stronger, fitter and more agile, the biggest gain from exercise is the hormonal transition from feeling a stressed, anxious and edgy person, to a calm, content and relaxed individual, resulting in a more pleasant existence. Allowing more control and more energy with a better-quality sleep routine, and more time can be spent on repairing and maintaining, rather than preparing to fight a tiger.

Start with exercise and everything else becomes that little bit easier.

Fresh Air

Mental health has become so much of a problem that it's even having an impact on global economics. At the time of writing, there are forty-two million people of working age in the UK. Statistics say that twelve million of these people struggle with regular mental health issues, and two million have regular sick periods from work because of it, and that's just in the UK. Globally, the estimation is that one in four people now experience some sort of mental health issue each year. That's close to two billion people, which is twice as much as five years ago in 2019.

So, what's changed? What's happened to make this devastating and dramatic change in our health? Basically, the Covid 19 pandemic. I know everyone is sick to death of hearing about it, but it has changed the world, our jobs, our relationships, our cultures, our pastimes, our attitudes, our finances and our perspectives. This isn't going away. This is the new world, and we haven't got a clue how to live in it.

The lockdowns obviously forced people to stay home for long periods of time, not knowing how dangerous it was going to be. The lockdowns also changed the way businesses performed, and in order for companies to stay alive they had to adapt overnight, very quickly developing the resources to allow their employees the ability to work from home. Pretty much instantly, people socialised, worked, shopped, exercised and created new hobbies that kept them safe in their homes. Unfortunately, after the lockdowns had passed, everyone continued with the same habits. Nobody went out and they became more and more reclusive, creating deeper and deeper health issues for themselves. When people did muster the courage to go outside and be around others, it created anxiety and a weariness that sent them running back to the safety of their screens. Even now, years later, I still feel the tension in a lot of people as I run around my town. There is a different energy, a nervous energy from many people when they are outside and among unfamiliar faces. Agoraphobia has suddenly become so much more of a problem. I know people who haven't been out for a couple of years. I teach someone in my studio who will only come out of her home to see me twice a week, and that is only if it's in the dark hours so no one can see her.

We have never had such a high percentage of the working population regularly absent from work, and this puts pressure on the employees who are managing to get to work every day. Regrettably, the remaining staff members are covering hours and shifts for the colleagues who aren't making it to work, so the workload keeps flowing and the company stays alive. This extra weight on their shoulders does eventually break them into submission, which then makes them require time off to recoup. It's a vicious and scary downward spiral that doesn't seem to have an answer and could have drastic effects on the future of all of us.

Along with the pandemic of obesity and diabetes, which is now advancing at such a speed that we have come to terms with the fact that the human body has a new form, we also now have a mental illness pandemic. We have a world that has one in four people suffering mentally and one in eight people struggling with obesity. One pandemic is feeding the other, and both are accelerating out of control because of people's inability or unwillingness to go outside and move. So many people never walk anywhere; not for any reason whatsoever as they find comfort and safety in the secure boxes of their homes, their work environment and their cars. They don't walk around a supermarket or to the local pub or coffee shop; they don't venture into a local field or park to just feel the breeze or to see open spaces; they never feel the freedom nature provides away from the straight lines we are controlled by every moment our eyes are open. Screens, doorways, rooms, supermarket aisles, even the white lines that guide us down the correct side of the road. These lines subliminally imprison us, trap us and direct us into a subdued way of thinking. They make us believe it's all there is, it's the only choice we have, we have to follow the line in order to stay safe; much like a worker ant.

Open spaces, big skies, random shapes, different smells, wind on our skin, the rustling of leaves and the crunch on the ground as your feet roll over it; even the taste of fresh air as it fills our lungs, all stimulate our senses, creating excitement and opportunity. Just sitting on a park bench for ten minutes can and will change your day, at least your perception of it. I'm not saying the answer to your problems is found in a country park, and I totally understand that shit will always be there, but the ability to handle the difficult times more efficiently and productively, definitely is. Awakening your suppressed senses can only happen when you reconnect to the one stable thing we have always had, and that's nature.

In my opinion, mental strength is built on two things; first, developing the ability to stand back up time after time, regardless of the knocks and kicks; and second, by open spaces. The mind needs the space to evolve, to learn from those kicks and those knocks and develop the skills that can get you back on your feet. It's medicine for your mind, far more effective than those little paralysing pills that are so freely dished out. It doesn't take long, just twenty to thirty minutes every day in all weathers. In fact, the harsh weather will stimulate the senses even more, creating excitement and an adrenaline surge. Fresh air and open space is the number one helping hand to get you through a difficult day, a difficult week or a difficult period. We all need to start rebuilding ourselves, one at a time, if we are to hand over any sort of life to our future generations.

So, there it is. My five pillars. Eat healthy, keep hydrated, sleep well, exercise, and get fresh air every day. This is what I look at when I'm a little broken. I'm 99% positive that if life isn't looking good, if you are struggling, feeling ill or not coping, then a pillar needs improvement. This is what I preach to my children relentlessly and annoyingly. Everyone who has ever spent more than an hour with me in my studio understands what I mean when I say, "Look at your pillars".

Chapter 6

Back on my feet.

The expected and triumphant completion of the 2023 6633 Arctic Ultra was going to be the grand finale to this book, the big Disneyesque romantic climax to this story, the typical American underdog finishing on top against all the odds. But, as always, plans tend to go sideways, life continues to remind you you're not in control, and in short, basically, shit happens.

Re-assessing and rebuilding my five pillars during the second half of 2023, helped me recover rapidly from the kicking I received in the frozen wilderness of northern Canada. By the end of the year, I was back on my feet and ready to charge into 2024 with a single mission, to find a conclusion to this story. Fitness was building, strength was growing, and most importantly my hunger had been reignited. I stood pigeon chested at the doorway of the new year ready to grab it by the balls and run with it. This was going to be THE year. I was excited, enthusiastic and eager to make shit happen. The weight from running my old gym was gone, and the studio was working and allowing me to have time back for myself. At the time I felt I had failed, but now I was back doing what I was supposed to be doing, working with clients privately on a 1-2-1 basis. For the first time in five years, I felt I was making a proper difference to people's lives. My family was happy and healthy, with both my girls growing fast and finding their own directions, and Teri showing a level of contentment with where she was in her world. The pressure of the Arctic had dispersed, and I sensed a freedom I hadn't felt for a long time. I was able to really knuckle down into my training, and in my fiftieth year I was comfortably smashing all my previous goals and personal bests.

All I had set myself as a personal challenge for the year was to create the last chapter of this book. Something awe inspiring, something dramatic and ridiculous, which would encourage and motivate others to grow and fight and be the best they could be. Now, there wasn't a chance in hell I was going to invest any more money into trying to finish the 6633 Arctic Ultra. Firstly, because of the unfairness and unprofessionalism I had felt there, but also because I honestly believe I would be looking at a divorce if I was to ask my wife for another pass at this, but I did want something which would make people stand up and take notice.

Whilst I was scrolling through the search engines and juggling a few options in the air, I noticed a growing interest around the running world, and in general news, of an ultra-running athlete called Jack Scott who was leading the biggest, hardest footrace in the UK called the Spine Race. He was absolutely smashing it and looked set to destroy the previous record. The previous one was set by a woman called Jasmin Paris, and was said to be unbeatable. This really caught my attention for a number of reasons, but mainly because it was very rare that an ultra-marathon race would make general news headlines. This widely covered interest from the general public made me believe this could be my next focus.

The Spine Race is classed as the ultimate ultra marathon race in the UK and categorised as one of the hardest in Europe. It's a 268-mile race up one of the longest public footpaths in the UK called the Pennine Way. It starts in Edale, a small village in Derbyshire, and finishes just over the Scottish border at the wall of a pub called The Border Hotel in Kirk Yetholm. The route has an elevation change of approximately 20,000 metres (65,000 feet) of ups and downs and follows England's rocky spine from the hills of the Derbyshire Peak District and the Yorkshire Dales, through the stunning Swaledale Valley, across the North Pennines, and over Hadrian's Wall in Northumberland to the Cheviot Hills. Some of the best scenery England can offer. There are two versions of the race, a summer and a winter. Both follow the same path, covering the 268 miles of the whole Pennine way; both have the same rules of having to carry with you the necessary safety essentials; food, water, hygiene and first aid from checkpoint to checkpoint. Your drop bag will then be taken to the next checkpoint for you to be restocked. On average each checkpoint is around 45-50 miles apart, so that's a long way to survive on your own, and a lot of luggage to carry on your back when the objective is to move as quickly as possible. You only have six days to finish the summer race, and six and a half days to finish the winter one. Even though the winter is classed as the hardest, which is why they allocate an extra twelve hours to finish, they both come with their unique challenges. The athletes running the winter version, which is set during the coldest month of January, have to endure deep bogs, heavy rain, gusting winds, blizzards and heavy snow, all with limited daylight hours as they are in darkness for sixteen to seventeen hours a day. Remember, this is a non-stop race on a very old, often unsigned and worn-out footpath that often disappears, so vigilance at all times is essential. The summer version does have a few things in its favour, such as eighteen hours of daylight, and a better climate as it is set in June and is generally harder and quicker under foot. But this heat brings its own challenges. Some of the reasons that people fail the summer race are heat stroke, as most races can reach a temperature of 30+ degrees Celsius, and insect bites, especially the midges and horse flies. I was nearly sent to hospital once because of a single horsefly bite on my calf when the swelling doubled the size of my lower leg. The midges - the bloody midges - are way worse than mosquitoes. They can become so overwhelming that they can send people mad when clouds of them, absolutely thousands of them, engulf you in a feeding frenzy as they simultaneously bite hundreds of times. Blisters from landing on the much dryer and harder surface from the overly-sweaty and swollen feet, and dehydration sets in because it's so hard to carry the water you need to get through the long, remote areas of the path, Some sections are very isolated, where you can go for hours and hours without seeing another human, or anything man made. They are both very, very difficult races in their own right.

As it was January, Jack Scott was cruising through the winter Spine Race, and I was in the middle of a mini first-world crisis, looking for something crazy to do this year that would be stupid enough to be worthy of my final chapter. Jack didn't just smash the record, he destroyed it by over ten hours, finishing in a superhuman time of 72 hours and 55 minutes in just a tad over three days. Three bloody days to do 268-miles, along with 20,000 metres of ups and downs in one of the coldest periods of winter we had experienced for a long time. Absolutely mind-blowing; hats off to you sir. This is why it made national news and was the talking point for people who didn't even know what an ultra-marathon was. To put the last piece of perspective on this achievement, Jasmin Paris broke the previous record last year of ninety-five hours, which had stood for six years, by twelve hours, by completing it in 83 hours and 12 minutes. As previously mentioned, this was said to be unbeatable, and then Scott comes along and destroys it.

I was in awe and buzzing from watching this event unfold, and with the country-wide acceptance of the difficulties and complexities of finishing this race, I knew this was my next adventure and a race worthy of the conclusion for my story. I signed up to the summer Spine Race by the end of the same day. The winter version was definitely making my hormones flow, but I couldn't wait for a year; I was too hungry. I'd go for the summer first and then jump on the winter next year.

Now I knew what the chequered flag looked like; I needed to make a plan to make sure I had the best chance of finishing. I still believed I was in the best running shape of my life, but hunger was hunger, and I wanted more. I had just under five months to make myself nigh on invincible and fully prepared for whatever the Spine would throw at me. I believed I had a 100-hour finish in me, which would put me in the top ten percent of finishers, because I know how quick I can move. My arctic adventures taught me that, along with how much sleep deprivation I can handle. So doing the maths, I knew that on a good day, a hundred hours is definitely within my capabilities. Sleep deprivation is an important skill in this race because one of the other rules is that racers are limited to six hours at each checkpoint. If you are not back out within six hours, you are out for good. Game over. That's an hour to refuel, clean, and fix all the injuries, four hours sleep and one hour to get set for the next stage. Four days of limited sleep whilst covering sixty-five miles a day is going to affect the head and the body. I also believe that, again by my calculations, in order to finish in a hundred hours, four hours sleep at each checkpoint is way too generous. I think it'll need to be more like two-three hours. Apparently, Scott survived on thirty mins sleep in the whole race, thirty mins in three days. Just bonkers, and way beyond my comprehension.

Within a week I had my plan. Every third weekend I would either be racing or spending the weekend rekeying the route, and the other weekends I would be covering thirty to fifty miles locally, as well as practising kit and food alternatives.

Badger Challenge

The first race in the calendar was a local one towards the end of February called the Badger Challenge. This is a six-hour endurance challenge consisting of as many laps as you can do in the time limit, around, up and over Beacon Hill. Each lap is approximately 3.4 miles with 460 feet of ascent. It's basically a challenge for all the local club runners to warm up the legs for the coming season, with around eighty participants. Beacon Hill is one of the most beautiful parts of Leicestershire, holding the status for the highest point of our shire, and surrounded by lovely woodland trails. It was a cold day with the temperature hovering around 5 degrees Celsius, and very wet and muddy under foot. Perfect conditions for practising for the heat of the summer, haha.

I felt strong at the beginning, completing my first lap with my good friend Ian who was there with his brother Lee; both very competent runners, standing well over six feet tall and seven to ten kilograms in weight less than me, also twenty years younger. My objective would be to hold my own with these fine specimens. After the first lap, Ian stopped briefly to adjust his shoes whilst I jogged on, knowing he would catch me before long. My plan was to be consistent. I've always gone off too quickly; I've always been the hare instead of the tortoise. I had to learn discipline in my running, so my plan was to find a comfortable pace and hold it throughout the six hours. As lap after lap went by, the plan was going well as the temperature dropped and it started raining, then some sleet and finally a brief flurry of snow. As I was about to complete my eighth lap, I came up to Lee who was about to finish his 7th. I couldn't believe it; I was about to lap Lee. I must be doing well, I thought. After a quick chat I stayed to my plan, which was to be steady and consistent, and run the whole six hours, so I continued forward. Ian never did catch me back up; in fact, I didn't see him again until I finished my 11th lap when he was standing at the finish line with Erica and Tom clapping me in as the six-hour time limit ticked by. He had just finished his 10th lap a few minutes in front of my 11th, so I had also beaten him by a whole lap. The eleven laps meant I had finished in 2nd place, having covered 37 miles and over 5,000 feet of rolling Leicestershire countryside, and I felt great. I could have continued for a couple more hours at that pace. Ian came in 5th and Lee 8th, both very respectable distances, and to be honest, where I was hoping to be on my best day. Erica also did amazingly well. With the support of her husband Tom, she completed her own personal challenge which was to complete the marathon distance of eight laps within the time limit, which she nailed with a good half an hour to spare. Challenge one completed and success for all involved.

The Amberaid Ultra Marathon

The next challenge on the calendar was 'The Amberaid Ultra Marathon', which was just over thirty miles of some of the most shittiest tracks I have ever raced on. Derbyshire really needed to keep this one hidden. But first I went to Edale to recce the Spine Race and covered the first sixty-five miles from the start line. It was the middle of March, and we had just had a whole winter's worth of rain in the past couple of weeks. The first day's target was forty-four miles, which finished at a small hostel for a few hours' sleep before an early rise and a quick twenty-one miles to see how the legs felt; then get a lift back from an old friend, Traycie, who lived close by.

I've spent many a sunny Sunday hiking the first part of this trail but have never seen such a mess. The bogs and mud were relentless. As soon as I made it through one, another appeared within minutes, each one hundreds of feet long. The weather once again was a mix of rain, wind, snow and sleet. The first day took me thirteen hours; three hours longer than expected, and unquestionably more painful than I was hoping for. My feet were a complete mess. I've felt a mess before, but not in this way; this felt different. As soon as I got into my room, which was luckily empty, I ordered a pizza and jumped into the shower. Feeling fresh, and with a belly full of Italian cuisine, I passed out, only to be woken sharply by my unsympathetic phone alarm a few hours later. I squeezed my tattered feet back into still-very-wet trainers, and I was on my way. Again, the terrain became instantly troublesome, and I was shin deep in floods and bogs. Sixteen miles into the day, the sun was shining for a change, and I was becoming a little sweaty. Stopping for a quick bite I re-assessed clothing which included a sock change. As I was replacing my socks, an old boy walked past with his dog, took one look at my feet and said, "This looks like the end of the road for you, son". What do you mean, I asked. "Your feet, my lad; you have trench-foot. I would get them looked after immediately before you really get into trouble". Never experiencing trench foot before, I did have a little panic and contacted Traycie straight away to collect me early, and that was my weekend adventure over. I should mention that, after a week or so the soles of both feet completely peeled off. It was something to behold, but no one else in the house seemed that appreciative of it when I showed them.

Onto the Amberaid. I stand by my words when I say this was one of the most unpleasant and crazy races, I have taken part in. I give all the credit to Ian for talking me into joining him and his brother, Lee. I should have had an inclination as to how bad it was going to be when I paid the entrance fee of just £25. The start was in this stinky yard of a pig farm. I realised that the farmer of this land was the organiser of the race when he strolled past the one hundred and ten runners dressed in wellies and a flat cap, with his two collie dogs by his side. This was definitely a runner's race. I felt like the oldest, the shortest and a little out of my depth. Everyone was dressed in top-end running attire, fingers quivering over their watches as they eagerly waited to get started before freezing to death. The farmer stood on an old worn-out tractor tyre as it lay on its side in its last resting place. We all stood facing him waiting for the usual health and safety speech. I wasn't expecting it to be so brief, but it went along the lines of

“Y’all ready then?” and a disheartened, nervous “Yep” came in response. “Ok then… GO”, he grumbled. We all stood there, not quite understanding the order. “GO, bloody GO”, he shouted, “down the hill over there”, as he pointed past the barn, “and I’ll see you in thirty-one miles”. We were strangely off, fighting for position as the first hundred yards was a bottle neck through ankle deep, slippery, churned-up mud from weeks and weeks of cattle being driven through it, destroying the ground we ran upon. I found out at the end of the race that this was as far as Ian made it into the race. He had a nasty slip, twisting his ankle and was out, having managed less than a minute of racing. I actually believe he probably got off lucky. That first few hundred metres set the precedent for the whole race. It was also a self-navigating race, as not a single clue or marker existed to say you were on the correct course. The first fourteen miles were through one bog after another: through hedges, over turnstiles, up and down small hills, and hitting a bog at the bottom of each hill. At the top of the highest hill, the wind was so strong the hail travelled sideways and felt like a thousand needles trying to puncture the skin at the same time. Then we hit a canal as everything flattened out and the legs were able to find a rhythm for the first time. After a few miles, I started to believe that we had conquered the challenging part of the course and relaxed into the race with a slight smile on my face. The sun was showing its face, the wind had died, and the legs were grateful for some continuity. After a few miles of pleasantly jogging along the canal and feeling pretty secure in my training, shit hit the fan again. I should have known that this bloody race had more to offer. With nine or ten miles remaining of the course, things turned stupidly nasty, as there wasn’t a single flat step left to enjoy. I was either going up or down the side of woodlands, and I mean frequently holding onto tree trunks to pull myself up the incline or sliding down the other side on my bum from one supportive tree trunk to another. The only respite from this monotonous repetition was the occasional pigs' wallow we had to negotiate through, whilst the pigs were still present and enjoying themself by burying their snouts deep in the sloshing, stinky, shitty mud. I have never felt anger on a race before, but this was stirring something red inside me. I found myself planning what I was going to say to Ian if I ever got to the end of this fucking ordeal. With less than a mile left my head started lifting, and just as my raised blood pressure started to subside, I very painfully realised I had strayed slightly off course. Only just, but I had missed a slight left turn about a mile back. Just when my blood pressure rose back up until steam started coming out of my ears, my legs spoke to me. Put in layman's terms, they basically said, "You can go to hell if you think I'm going back down there". So instead, I decided to turn instantly left and wade through the heavy vegetation and trees until I got to what looked like the road I should have been on. It couldn't be more than a couple of hundred metres, and I was right, it actually wasn't. Within a few minutes of dragging myself through thorn bushes, climbing over fallen trees, and sliding down muddy banks, I was within ten metres of the route. I knew it was the route because I saw another competitor wobble past. The problem was, to get there I needed to cross a waist deep stream, scramble through ten feet of thorns and stinging nettles, and climb over a six-foot drystack wall. There was no hesitation; it just happened. As a result of all the scratches and stumbles, I was already leaking more blood than I had done in any other race, and I looked and stunk like I had come out of the back end of one of those pigs. I really didn't care anymore. Job done, over the wall, and back into something that looked like a hobbling jog, trying to catch the runner who overtook me. Closer and closer I got with every stride until I could feel the anger and frustration coming from him too. Because of the stench coming from both of us, I must have been nose blind to the smell coming from the biggest source of squalor in the whole race. When we turned sharply out of the woodland and onto a steep embankment pointing skyward, we both fell into a bloody pit! Trying to conquer this pig's village meant spending time on our hands and knees struggling to get some tracking as we climbed two feet and slid down one. I did manage to catch the young lad who was trying to hold onto his three-meter lead on me at the turnstile as we exited the field, though. As my fellow masochist climbed over, both his legs cramped; they literally locked up. I could have taken advantage of this but decided to give him my shoulder to support him the last two hundred metres to the finish line. My bloody mistake, because within spitting distance of the finish line the lanky shithead sprinted off in front of me to claim 9th place; what an arsehole. He didn't even stop to say thanks after he crossed the line; he was gone. Ian was there, though, and did he get a mouthful from me? .... Well, I was going to, but I just didn't have it in me anymore. I just gave him the biggest, smelliest and shittiest hug I could, and retreated back to my van to assess the damage that was hidden beneath all the different shades of brown.

Manchester Marathon

A few weeks later and the Manchester Marathon came quicker than I expected. Mid-April, and I was hungry for a run that wouldn't end in trench foot, cuts and bruises or a bath in pig shit. The weather was near perfect, a bit chilly with a dampness in the air. I'd travelled up really early as I couldn't sleep, so I thought I would take the pressure off the long drive.

My original objective in running the Manchester Marathon was to qualify for the Boston Marathon in America. This is a marathon that pretty much only allows the fastest of each age category in the race. Each age category has what's called a 'good for age' time they must beat, allowing them to enter the ballot. The ballot is just a lottery to see if your name is drawn out to run the race. Then, when all the applications are in, there will be a time announced saying how much quicker than your 'good for age' you needed to be to get a place in the race. I had never managed a qualifying time before, so I originally intended for this to be the focus for my running year and to really push for speed. Being my 50th year, I would receive an extra five minute leniency on my 'good for age' qualification time, which now stands at 3 hours and 25 minutes. My personal best in a marathon was four years ago in London at 3 hours 33 minutes. I started this year working speed drills to get ready for today, but it wasn't long before I decided to enter the summer Spine Race which speed training had no business being part of. The Spine is an endurance game, so this marathon just became a practice day to enjoy and receive a bit of bling, and that's how I was going to approach it. Just enjoy it, I thought.

Standing at the start, shivering, I became overwhelmed with the enormity of this race. I hadn't really researched it; I had just looked at what my start time was and where I needed to be. There were 25,000 athletes shivering with me, including some global top-end professional runners, all of us looking for personal bests or even world records. This marathon is known for being a fast race because it's virtually flat, which is why I thought at the time that, if I was to qualify for Boston, this was the race to try.

The air horn erupted, play was pressed on my nineties R&B playlist, and my watch was woken up. We were off very quickly, proceeding along a very wide road allowing everyone to find their space within a few strides. I felt released and free as the first few miles quickly disappeared. I'd been covering distances of thirty to fifty miles on weekends, so my endurance was unquestioned; and I had been training mostly through trails, mud and bad weather, so this kind weather and tarmacked running surface, felt strange, almost like a breath of fresh air. Checking my progress at the ten-mile marker, I was averaging 7 min 42 sec per mile. Too fast for my uneducated-for-speed legs, but I felt comfortable, so I zoned out into the world of Snoop Dog, Dr Dre, Eminem and 50 Cent. Mile after mile flew past as I glided along trying to ignore the little buzz, I got from my watch to tell me I'd accomplished another mile. Mile 20, then 21 and 22, till I couldn't resist any more, so I glanced at my watch. I was still running at 7.42 per mile. I knew the speed I needed to enter the ballot for Boston was 7 min 49 sec per mile, so I was in the game and still feeling great. Head down and counting steps became the focus. I count steps a lot to occupy the voices that keep me company in my head. For example, I know that when I have jogged 1,480 steps, I've covered a mile. The voices weren't talking much, to be honest, but being proactive and giving them a job to do before they woke up couldn't hurt. Turning the last corner with a short sprint to the finish, I could see the timing clock ticking away and knew that, even if I crawled the last fifty metres I would achieve my 'good for age', but I held my pace and crossed the line with my hands punching the sky in a couple of seconds off 3 hours 22 minutes, three minutes inside my qualifying age time. Amazing! I was so, so chuffed with myself, and strangely felt like I had been on a training run. Pigeon-chested, I strolled through the exit gates, collecting my medal, t-shirt and goodies. I couldn't wait to call Teri to let her know I had done 'a thing'.

Examining the results of my efforts on Garmin, the most amazing recognition jumped out at me. Throughout the whole 26.2 miles of the race, my pace only changed by nine seconds per mile. Every mile was pretty much identical. In fact, my first five miles showed only a one-second difference to the last five miles. Near as damn it to the perfect race. Unfortunately, I didn't make Boston because there was a lot of speed that year, and even though I reached the ballot, I still wasn't quick enough. I was three minutes inside the age category, but everyone who qualified was at least 6 minutes 21 seconds quicker than their prospective 'good for ages'. I was still absolutely over the moon with such a perfect race, though. It was only April, and I had already smashed three races. Things were going well.

UTS100km

My glory in Manchester had to be brushed to the side, just for a bit, because three weeks later I was in Wales nervously anticipating the start of the UTS100km. This was undoubtedly the toughest single day race I had ever stood at the start line of. I had a right to be nervous. The distance wasn't the problem, obviously being 100km, which is normally my bag, but the total elevation change was 12,800 metres or 42,000 feet. I say again, 12,800 metres of ups and downs. I had been trying to increase my mountain-goat muscles by venturing into the local hills and throwing myself into stupid shitty races, deliberately looking for the worst, wettest and most boggy environments in which to ruin my weekends. But this is Wales, known for being unforgiving, aggressive and wet. I'd been checking the weather report for the two weeks approaching the big day and reading comments from racers in the online event chat groups who had been practising on the route. The weather was described as unpredictable; a mixture of sun, rain, big winds, sleet and maybe snow on the peaks, and the route; wet, muddy and boggy in the valleys. Precisely the conditions I had been fully immersing myself in, so I felt as prepared as I could be.

As I gently closed the front door of my house early Friday morning so as not to wake anyone, I thought to myself that I hadn't felt butterflies like this before a race for such a long time. The drive was a good three and a half hours which gave me plenty of time to visualise the weekend, and to come to terms with the fact that the weather had dramatically changed. As of the previous night's weather report, there was now going to be an unpredicted three-day heat wave. Not a bloody cloud in the sky, with temperatures touching 30 degrees Celsius. This is Wales, it's supposed to be wet and muddy, not the bloody Mediterranean. The first peak on the race is Snowdon, the biggest mountain in Wales and England. I had previously tamed Snowdon well over twenty-five times and only came down dry twice. I wasn't prepared and hadn't trained for the heat. I'm naturally not built for it. I am useless at it. I'm too muscular for heat. I'm not really even built to be a runner if I'm honest. Runners, good runners are generally very thin with great type two muscle fibres. These are the muscles for endurance. They don't require much energy or water; they are slender and are designed for slow continued use requiring little support. They evolved to cover large distances on the savannas of Africa hundreds of thousands of years ago when we would hunt our prey without the need of nourishment. I wasn't built like that. I had too many type 1 muscle fibres. They are the power muscles, the muscles that are there for fighting, climbing, swimming, lifting and carrying. These muscles hold a lot of moisture and require food to keep working optimally. Without continued hydration they will cramp very quickly.

So, here's a fun fact. I have never finished a race when the temperature has surpassed 30 degrees, except one, and that was the Milton Keynes Marathon a few years ago, when I spent the last five miles of the race being sick and enjoying regular diarrhoea-inspired pit stops in hedges.

After going through the kit check, etc, I spent a few hours lying on the grass soaking up as much of the already scorching sun whilst sipping litre after litre of water filled with electrolytes, trying to accumulate as much as possible. I was waiting to meet a couple called Alex and Anuj who were allowing me to rent a sofa bed off them for the weekend in their holiday rental to save us both a little money. He was from Cyprus and also in the same distance race as me. Anuj was from Slovenia and just starting to build up her running CV, although this weekend felt a bit too much. She was very supportive and welcoming and instantly made me feel part of the little group. We spent a nice day together eating some lovely home cooked food which they considerately shared with me, and shared stories into the late hours. This lateness bit us in the arse because we needed to be up and out by 4am for our 5am start time.

Arriving at the start area with a slightly hungover feeling, although no alcohol was consumed, we entered an arena of loud music and big lights to take away the darkness that still hung over the morning's anticipation. A few hundred lunatics stood, heads down, goosebumps displayed and bowels twitching in the nervousness of a very difficult day ahead. With thirty seconds left, it was a tradition for all competitors to sing along with the race's shanty song to build the occasion. Then the siren suddenly eclipsed all other noise, sending us on our way into the murkiness and to experience the mysteries ahead. One thing that wasn't going to be a mystery was the expected heat as the sun rose.

The first climb was straight up and over Snowdon. This was the first of two visits to the top of this iconic landmark as we would be here again at around the 48-ish mile marker. The view at the top was perfectly timed because I was lucky enough to witness the sun casting beams of light over the surrounding mountains. It was uplifting and almost audible, I swear I could hear the day waking up. I hit the first support station at Pen-y-pass on the other side of Snowdon two hours and fifteen minutes into the race. I was deliberately taking it extra cautiously because of the anticipated approaching heat, holding myself back a little whilst continually supping on the three litres of liquid I was carrying, but this was all consumed before I hit the 8-

mile first checkpoint. Two sandwiches and two brownies inhaled, and the bladder topped to the brim, I left to hit another 800 metre vertical climb. The view in front was of a 200-person caterpillar-like chain zigzagging up the wall of rocks in front of me, with only one footstep between each athlete. Cresting the top meant we all came out of the shadow of the mountain and felt the heat of the day cascade over us for the first time, instantly making every pore of my skin leak. Scrambling down the 800 metres drop on the sunny side using hands, bum, knees and elbows, I started to come to terms with the fact that this wasn't a running race, it was a climbing race. As soon as we hit the bottom of the valley it was straight back up again, and over another 600-metre bump. This needed conquering before the second checkpoint could be seen. With only fifteen miles of the race done, we had already climbed and dropped 2,200 meters, way over 7,200 feet. Arriving at the second aid station just in time as I had just finished another three litres of liquids. This checkpoint was very well stocked with every variety of food and drink you would expect at such a high-level running event. I spent a good twenty minutes devouring everything I could and washing it down with a couple of coffees. Refilling my liquids and carrying an extra litre in my hand, I launched myself back into the oven. We were told there was a bit of a cock-up at the next checkpoint as the landowner had changed his mind and would not allow the event organisers to place a resting place on his land. In other words, there was a checkpoint missing, making what would have been the 4th checkpoint, now the 3rd, and creating a longer section of sixteen miles. In this heat and adding another 1,000 metres of climbing and descending to the race tally, it was going to make this sixteen-mile chunk very tough. My first thought was, I'm going to need to slow right down and be very conservative with my four litres of water. But, as careful as I was, I still ran out after about twelve miles, instantly becoming dehydrated. The temperature was touching the mid 30's in the valleys and I was dripping, even at the walking pace I was managing to maintain. I was on the only flat section of the race and couldn't even muster a steady jog. I was dropping, legs were heavy, lungs tight and mind drifting. I'm still shocked today at how quickly my body disintegrated in that temperature. I even rang Teri for some support because I was starting to panic through the dehydration. I passed numerous athletes on the ground in the foetal position, crying and shivering with people around them worryingly trying to help, keeping them calm and forcing them to remain in the small, isolated pieces of shade. A few hundred feet further on there were friends of competitors and volunteers running past in the opposite direction with bottles of water for the collapsed racers behind me. I was getting dizzy and started to feel like I might go down. Still on the phone with my wife and at breaking point, I was about to say I'm going down, I'm done, when an image of a small tent appeared a hundred feet in front. A water station, a bloody water station. 'Fucking A'. I was saved. I shuffled into the tent and poured two bottles of water down my throat in seconds. A third bottle full of electrolytes helped down some brownies, the only nutrition available, and I started to reconnect. I felt so relieved, instantly feeling better about life. We had less than two miles until the official checkpoint, and this was the biggie; the big halfway checkpoint. A fully loaded buffet with hot and cold foods and drinks as well as our drop bags, so I could get some fresh new clothes on. This was the only thing

I was thinking about for the last two hours; a much-needed reset.

I stumbled into the local village hall, which was gratefully lent to us as the halfway checkpoint, nine hours into the race, feeling like I had just crossed the Sahara Desert. There were bodies everywhere, in all kinds of conditions; people shaking, crying, sleeping, and most staring into oblivion as if frozen in time. There were blood-stained plasters and bandages everywhere, a few puddles of vomit which needed dodging, and volunteers running around hysterically trying to cope with the onslaught. Everywhere stunk of vomit, pee and sweat, which didn't make the willingness to grab some food very inviting, especially when I found out the warm food of choice for the event was curry. Yep, you read that correctly - curry! It was over 30 degrees Celsius, everyone was dehydrated, hurting, bleeding and being sick. We had covered a very hard 31 miles and climbed over 11,000 feet, 3,500 metres thus far, and they supplied light brown, runny Chinese-type curry. The smell alone made me throw up everything I had consumed at the water station two miles back. I was on my knees and now shouting 'Ralph' to the already accumulated cocktail of vomit on the toilet floor. The floor was the only place to do it because every toilet was blocked with more of the stuff. This wasn't the oasis I was dreaming of as I meandered through the last sixteen miles. I was in a mess, we all were. I managed to find myself a dry, quietish spot and steadily changed into fresh clothes whilst nibbling on my own snacks and sipping on a few cups of extra-sugary tea. Every fibre of my being was saying this is stupid, I'm done, let's get the hell out of here. But an hour and a half later I stumbled to my feet and squeezed my way out of the building and up the road.

Nine miles to the next checkpoint and, just like it had been written in stone, it was straight up another 800-metre climb. The heat was relentless. It seemed as soon as I put liquids in, they evaporated away. I started to realise I had drunk around twelve to thirteen litres of water so far and still hadn't taken a pee. This fifth big climb was unbearable. I was driven to my bum or knees every hundred metres. I was playing yo-yo with other racers as we took it in turns hitting the dusty ground, unable to progress any further forward until we'd had a small reprieve, before fighting our way back to our feet to retake the positions we'd lost as others were collapsing for a few minutes rest.

I can't remember much about reaching the summit of this mountain. It obviously happened because I was descending; not very well but descending. I remember struggling to walk straight and tripping over rocks a few times. I remember a nice grassy meadow as part of the descent, and I can remember people talking to me on occasion, but the next thing I vividly remember was lying in an ambulance with straps over me and a paramedic talking to me as he checked my vitals.

Apparently, I was staggering across a road a mile or so away from the checkpoint asking everyone for directions. A couple walking their dog took me under their wing and escorted me to the next checkpoint and to the ambulance, where they explained my situation to the paramedic. Apparently when the paramedic was talking to me whilst trying to take a blood sample, I became aggressive and took a few swings at him, which is why I was strapped to the bed. Not my greatest hour, but in my defence, I wasn't present.

Other than what I've said, I can't remember a single thing about the ordeal.

The ambulance drove me back to the start-finish line where I spent the next three hours being looked after and brought back into the land of the living. This is where I finally learnt my body shape isn't designed for this weather. It requires too much water to feed my type 1 muscle fibres. The head medic on the race 'Jonny' - yes, my mate Jonny who was the medic on the 6633 Arctic Ultra - explained he had been treating everyone with my body shape all day and was fully anticipating my arrival.

This event was the conclusion of my training for the Spine race, and that's how I approached the event. It wasn't my be-all and end-all to the year; it was merely a very, very hard training day, meant to break me and to hopefully extend my limitations and thresholds. It certainly did that. I knew from the first second I saw the weather the day before that it was going to change the outcome, but I was determined to get everything I could from it. So, job done, and onto the main event.

Chapter 7

Show a little backbone

Who would have thought it? Three months of training in temperatures close to freezing; marching, running and enduring high winds, heavy rain, sleet, snow, mud, bogs and pig shit, to end up running the first major race of the year in what turned out to be the hottest weekend of the year. As soon as I saw that weather report the day before, I knew I was in for a battle, but I'm just putting it down to bad luck. I give myself credit to have earned and fully deserved to stand on that start line. I had done the miles, the pre races, and practised nutrition and hydration; I had bought the correct gear and was in the best mind set. It just wasn't to be that time.

I didn't have time to dwell on it as I only had four weeks until the main event of the year, the Summer Spine Race of 268 miles with 10,700 or 35,000 feet of ascent, and it needed to be done within six days. The course had only five checkpoints and these would be limited to a maximum stay of six hours. This might sound adequate to get a nice rest, but after an hour of food and recovery and an hour of prep for the next stage, there are only four left to close your eyes. That's if you decide to use the full quota of hours as most don't. I was actually planning on sleeping for only two hours at each opportunity. After all, I was looking for a 100-hour finish. If I used the whole six hours at each resting point, I would only have seventy hours to move over the 268 miles. If I only stayed for four hours at each checkpoint, I would give myself an additional ten hours of moving time.

I had built this race up in my head a bit, but I believed it warrantied the concern. This wasn't an easy trail. It covered a very lengthy portion of the English countryside as it snaked its way up the backbone of middle earth. There isn't much flat land, and the route can get a little confusing at times. Vigilance is necessary at all times, because not only will you lose precious time if you have to retrace your steps, but you also receive time penalties for coming off route. This awareness can be hard to maintain when sleep deprivation kicks in. Also, I know it's only the UK, but there are little bloody beasties that can stop your race. Because of the heat of summer and the bogginess of the route, the midges will be out in their millions, accompanied by an army of mosquitoes, and my arch enemy, the horse fly. I have been bitten by these little fuckers a few times, and every time they have nearly hospitalised me. I have heard plenty of stories of people losing limbs because of these. However, I did feel confident about my expectations of a finish, and hopefully within my time parameters. I could once again be proud of the fact that I had prepared perfectly. I'd done the miles, practised sixty percent of the route, had the right gear, and knew exactly how to look after my nutrition and hydration. My drop bag was militarily organised as I had included everything I had learnt in the Arctic, and the weather was looking favourable for me. A comfortable temperature with light winds and a few drops of rain each day. I had noticed, though, that June was already the wettest June in thirty years, but I presumed that, even with the quantity of rain that had fallen in the past couple of weeks, it still wouldn't be anywhere near as bad as when I was practising the route in February and March. This was also said to have added up to being the wettest winter for years. I had spent most of these winter months living in these torturous bogs, weekend after weekend.

It was a 9am start on a miserable, grey and rainy Sunday morning in a small, but very well-known village called Edale. Teri had made the two-hour drive with me to see me off and provide me with a smiley face to lift me up and give me some confidence. There were around 120 Spiners standing on the start line, and I stood nervously stalking around the middle of the pack. I tried my hardest to keep an eye on Teri as she grinned forcefully through the worry and heavy rain. When racers are in the last moments before a starting gun is fired, standing there with anticipation under the arch waiting to be set free to do their victory lap, they mentally checklist everything they have bought, learned, trained, and practised. They make sure they have done everything possible to ensure a successful adventure, visualising all the boxes, and mentally checking they have all been ticked over the past few months. Then in seconds, filtering through every aspect of the race preparations one last time. From training plan to the pre-race cool down; from kit choice to food choice; from racing strategy to understanding how to overcome unpredictable problems and untrainable entities that might arise during the event. This is exactly what I was doing as I stared in Teri's direction, soaking up her nervous excitement, and proud energy. I satisfactorily concluded I had done everything I could possibly have done to make this a happy ending. I had done the first 80% of the work perfectly. Everything over the past few weeks and months had gone as planned; well, apart from the

Snowdonian Sauna four weeks ago. I just had the last 20% left, which was to run up the backbone of England in six days. This, I confidently whispered to myself, I can do. This is what I'm good at. This is who I am and why I do what I do. I'm a relentless plodder, emotionlessly placing one foot in front of the other with no care for why. The only thing that could make this job even slightly better, I thought, was if I had a running buddy, someone with the same speed and same approach as me, someone to share stories with and who was easy to talk to.

It turned out that his name was also Stuart. He was shivering next to me, also waiting to be released from his overthinking. He thought I was talking to him when I whispered, "this I can do", as he replied "Sorry, I didn't hear you". This sparked a conversation that continued for, well, actually, hours. We set off together, not really feeling the adrenaline or hearing the starting gun. We just broke into our natural stride when some space appeared in front of us. I waved and blew a kiss to Teri amid chatter with Stuart and proceeded in the pouring rain to the foot of the first climb, which was around 600 metres up Jacob's ladder to Kinder Scout. The conversation flowed as well as the rain, and the first ten miles went swimmingly; and I meant that literally. Everywhere was flooded. For the first fifteen or so miles, as we ran out of the Peak District, there was a well-laid stepping-stone path, perfect for jogging along. Once we'd peaked Kinder Scout, the legs were able to be stretched a little and we picked up a bit of speed. Caution was definitely the name of the game in this section though, because as mentioned, floods were everywhere, and sometimes they were deep enough not to be able to see the stepping stones, and to miss them would mean landing a few inches lower and creating a dangerous trip hazard. Unfortunately, this did happen to one of the favourites to win the race. We passed him a couple of hours into the day, and he had with him an entourage of helpers assessing his leg because it was pointing in the wrong direction halfway down his shin. His foot had landed in a gap between two flat paving stones, a good 25-30 cm below the waterline, and with his very efficient travelling speed he continued moving forward, snapping his shin - yowch!. This visual reminder to take it easy provoked an on-going safety discussion between Stuart and myself and probably led to the elephant in the room question, 'How quickly do you think you can do this race?'. This is a bit of a taboo question amongst ultra runners, but we were a few hours into our chatting and storytelling, so I thought I would go for it. He smiled awkwardly and said he believed a hundred hours was doable. I immediately replied to this with a smirk, to which he took a little offence because he thought I was laughing at his optimism. Sensing this I very quickly continued by rolling off all the times I thought I could make each checkpoint by and how long I would rest and recoup at them, all the way to the finish line, bringing me in at around ninety-eight hours. With a shocked look on his face, he shoved his hand into the front pocket of his coat to retrieve a laminated piece of paper and handed it to me. Unfolding it, it revealed, as close as damn it, exactly what I had just described to him. We both had exactly the same game plan. With a little nod of the head, a contented side smile and a fist bump, we agree to support each other through the difficult times, lift each other when needed and walk across the finish line straight into the local pub together. Onward and upward, I thought, as I played through the sentence I had thought at the start line: the only thing that could make this journey better and easier would be to find someone with the same speed and same approach as me, someone to share stories with and who was easy to talk to. Well, as luck would have it, here he was another Stuart.

Stuart was a few years older than me, a lot taller and had a few quality races already under his belt, although this was also his first attempt at a Spine race. He currently lived in Inverness but came from the London area. He seemed very confident in his abilities and his plan and gave off a calmness and sense of control. Perfect for spending a five-day adventure with.

The rain was persistent, but at least the variation of rain kept us on our toes. Sometimes it was heavy, sometimes misty, sometimes it seemed to focus on a specific area; it was like the adjustable water hose adapter I have in the garden. It was mostly straight down on the lower grounds, but a jet power washer on the high grounds as the wind howled it into our sides, occasionally forcing a stumble. This was bloody June for goodness' sake; this was supposed to be the 'Summer Spine race'. This is the race where they take twelve hours off the maximum finishing time because it's supposed to be a bit easier to progress, a bit dryer under foot. The winter version of the race is renowned to be bog after bog, flood after flood, with continuous rain and winds. The environment is tough on the winter race because of the exact racing conditions we are now experiencing in June, but we weren't necessarily kitted up for these conditions. This was starting to affect both our moods, but we continued with the positive talks and 'getting to know you' stories as we slid, marched, crawled, and nearly swam through some of the floods and bogs. The number of times we went onto our arses or needed to get on our hands and knees to drag ourselves through the mud and peat, we should have looked like we'd been in a mud-wrestling competition, but the rain kept us relatively clean. Stories and statistics were starting to work their way through the grapevine that more people had already withdrawn or been pulled out of the race in the first twelve hours than the whole of last year's race. One of these withdrawals was another favourite to win, and they had found it necessary to take him to the hospital because of blisters, bloody blisters. This was someone who raced for a living and was sponsored by one of the leading running-shoe companies. How bad must the blisters have been for a professional to need a hospital visit, especially on the first day?

Anyway, step after step and breath after breath we continued. Oblivious to the seconds, minutes and hours rolling by until we suddenly and surprisingly stumbled into the first checkpoint mid-story. It was pitch black with a heavy cloud cover and, predictably, it was still raining. We had covered the forty-four miles only three minutes behind the predicted arrival time on Stuart's laminated sheet of paper. It was three minutes past 10pm when we stepped, joyfully, into the comfort of this checkpoint. Mostly joyous anyway, as it had definitely been a tough one and had felt longer than forty-four miles.

Now, when you take into account that I have previously raced approximately eighty races of marathon distance and above, and had sat in hundreds of checkpoints, I have to say with my hand on my heart that this was the best checkpoint I had ever stepped into and had the privilege to experience. Approaching it, I could hear my race number being shouted like Chinese whispers through the pitch-black wooded area, so my drop bag had been found and was already on a volunteer's back as he prepared for my arrival around the last corner and into the entrance to the hall. He guided me to a clean, spacious area whilst carrying my bag for me, and then set it perfectly in place for easy access. Within seconds, another volunteer asked which hot drink I would like, and another asked whether I wanted chili con carne or risotto, to which I replied both, and some of that jam roly poly with custard, please, that I could see across the room. Another volunteer came to see if I needed help removing my wet socks and clothes, etc, and to find towels and dry clothes from my bag. Once that was done, she assessed me for any medical issues that needed attending to. I was shocked, impressed and honoured to have received the efficiency and care they showed towards everyone who came through those doors. I was like a Formula one driver pulling into the pits. Amazing. It lifted both Stuart and myself so much that we were ready to rock and roll again within the hour, fully recovered, cleaned, dried, with full stomachs and pumped with caffeine. We very quickly decided to skip the sleep part and head straight back out into June's winter weather.

The next section was the longest of the race at just over seventy miles until checkpoint 2, so we made the decision to get a head start and mosey on through the night. The rain and wind had now escalated, and we knew it was going to be a long night. We left the checkpoint in a valley, so anticipated a solid climb out. The wind was already throwing its weight around and within minutes we were dripping again. However, it was what we expected so we persisted forward. As mentioned, many times before, I'm not the best during the dark hours. Having Stuart around was a bit of a saviour, but I still asked if I could put some music in my ears as a distraction, to which he gratefully agreed, saying it would be nice to lose ourselves for a few hours. As we crested the climb, I knew we had just started the Yorkshire Dales, a massive expanse of moorland. We couldn't see a thing, even with the head torches trying to force a way through. I could only just see Stu's feet a few metres in front of me, partly because of the rain coming at us from the side, partly because the wind wouldn't allow me to lift my head with any conviction, and partly because his feet kept disappearing under flooded swamps.

Listening to a mixture of Meat Loaf, Queen, Bon Jovi and Genesis, I tried to ignore the fact that every mile felt like ten, and it would take forty minutes to wade through a mile of this marshland. The mud continued to increase, and the water in places became knee deep which made remaining somewhere near the path impossible. Fighting against the driving wet sheets of rain, I occasionally tried lifting my head to have a look around in the hope I would see any glimmer of a reprieve from this torture. I could see the odd glimmer of light from a head torch in front and a couple of faint glows behind, and the wind would carry the voices of other racers struggling through this stupidity. I'd hear a splash and then "For fuck's sake", and then from another direction, "Thats, it, I've had enough of this shit, I'm finished with this". You'd sometimes see a head torch suddenly disappear into the ground and then reemerge as the owner of it shouted or growled or screamed at the darkness. It was becoming a bit ridiculous. I swear my feet hadn't come out of water for a good hour or so, and they hadn't taken more than four consecutive steps without slipping to one side or another, causing a stumble that needed three steps to recover from. Then I would be stumbling, slipping or tripping on something else. I was slowly turning into the hulk through rage. The music was even switched off and put away because Phil Collins was pissing me off.

Then it happened; a stumble that turned into a full-on fall. I face planted; well, belly flopped into the water, totally scuba diving the occasion. Stuart later said he heard a splash, looked behind him, and there was nothing apart from my rucksack floating on the water, so he grabbed it, then realised I was still attached. Stumbling back to my feet with the assistance of the big man, I was in a mess. Muddy, boggy water all over me, inside every item of clothing, in my mouth and eyes, under my hat, and over the headtorch. I couldn't see a bloody thing. I instantly started shaking beyond control. I knew I was in trouble, but also knew that this wasn't the place to consider how much trouble I was in. We cautiously moved forward, trying to secure every footing before relying on it to prevent another fall. I really don't know how many times I went swimming. The next mile was the most horrendous I have ever endured. I couldn't see or hear anything. Even the Arctic hadn't made me feel this cold. I was numb and could quite easily have just given up. I would have been content with lying down where I was and going to sleep if it hadn't been for Stu calmly dragging me forward. At some point there was another guy next to me. I don't know when he arrived, where he came from or how long he had been there, but he too started encouraging me forward, demanding I take another step. This is exactly what I did. I took another step, and then just one more, and another. Even though I couldn't see or feel anything I just started counting my steps, adding up how many steps it was until I reached safety. I did notice that this new guy encouraging me forward seemed a bit strange, because he wasn't dressed like a runner. He had a massive winter coat and wellies on and looked relatively fresh. He repeated himself over and over, encouraging me by saying we are nearly there, we can get you sorted out in a few more minutes. I was confused, I thought he must be losing it because we were in the middle of nowhere, five miles from the nearest village, and still 60 ish miles from the next checkpoint where my drop bag would be with a set of dry clothes in it. Sixty miles, that thought distracted my counting, sixty miles before I can rebuild from this. How could I make that distance like this? I'm really screwed, I thought.

Suddenly I heard noise; I heard conversation. Lifting my head I saw lights and strangely smelt food. What was going on? I really had lost my marbles. This wasn't a mirage, it was real. I went round a hedge and there was a big bonfire and two big tents. Someone was cooking sausages on a BBQ under the tent, and there were chairs and the smell of coffee. People scuttling about like working ants in hi-vis vests looking after all the injured souls who were covered in blankets and holding hot water bottles. Shocked, I stood in the middle of this chaos before a couple of volunteers came charging towards me, stripped me to my underwear, sat me down and smothered me in blankets and hot bottles of water until my face was the only thing showing from within the cocoon.

Mountain rescue had decided to build their support station at the end of this 4-5-mile-long swamp. Because they had been called to the area so much over the past few days. It was easier and more efficient to stay. I sat in that chair for three hours, constantly being force-fed sausage cobs and cups of tea in the hope I would soon be able to lift my body temperature.

Hyperthermia had set in. I couldn't hold a conversation, move any muscles, stop shaking, or focus on anything in front of me for nearly three hours. I wasn't alone. Every few minutes another stray would wander through the entrance equally damaged, some crying, some bloody, but all looked like they had just crawled out of the trenches in a war.

Unfortunately for me, Stuart was sent on his way. He did try to stay but wasn't permitted. The rules of the race stated that you could only stop at an unofficial resting place for a maximum of two hours before disqualification. I had been in this chair, being nursed back to humanity, for three hours, so I assumed I was out. I started to accept this as my reality, that was until a member of the rescue team told me they didn't have the authority to exit me from the race, and I would need to have a chat with race officials to see what fate they would decide for me. My ears pricked up. There was hope, and I made myself look as well-presented as I could for the video call.

The call started with a ten-minute, slow and delicate, common-sense, description of how it would be irresponsible of them to allow me to continue. But with the power of my words, I managed to persuade them ... no, correct that, not persuade, I begged them to let me continue. They agreed on one condition, that I spent the next ten miles with someone just in case the hyperthermia returned. Apparently, if hyperthermia only lasts for an hour or so, it could just be a blip and, hopefully, recoverable, but if it goes on for hours, it could mean it's gone deeper and may return at any time in the next few days. Hearing these terms and conditions which would give me a return into the race, two of the most considerate men instantly said "we'll take him with us, if that's ok". "Excellent, that's just perfect, thank you so much," I enthusiastically replied, to the two guys, and jumped up out of the camping chair with all the pizzazz of a sloth, instantly sitting back down, as if I wanted to, and not because I very quickly realised, I needed to.

With a little help I was dressed in my dry but stinky clothes, dry because they had spent the last couple of hours next to the bonfire, and stinky because they had spent the last couple of hours drying out next to the bonfire, and added to that, the unquestionable stench of a wet moorland cocktail. It wasn't too long before I found myself placing one foot in front of the other again and I was back in the race with my new compadres. Slowly and steadily, we progressed through the next few miles. The sun was glimmering occasionally from behind the high clouds, there were no more bogs for now, and I had some company. I did miss Stuart though and was hoping he was ok. I didn't really have any energy for conversation, and it was nice to just dawdle behind the other two listening to their chit chat. I was struggling with the cold a bit but didn't let on. I was dressed in all my cold-weather gear; including gloves and a hat, whilst they were both down to shorts, long-sleeve shirts and a baseball cap. I knew I was still feeling the cold and I knew that this wasn't a good sign. After a few miles I needed some space. I needed to figure out how I was going to get through the next fifty-five miles and to my drop bag, when I'm still only travelling at a couple of miles per hour, and I'm wearing everything I have left that is dry. Even when I could shake my helpers and speed up a bit, I still needed to get through another night.

We reached a small village about ten miles further on from the mountain rescue camp, and through an Oscar-level acting performance, I explained to my companions that I now felt great. I was going to sit on a wall, grab something to eat and have a quick reset of my clothes. I insisted I wouldn't be far behind them, and I would catch them up shortly. I was actually in a bit of a hole, and I sat there trying to find a way through this situation. All I needed to do was get to the checkpoint, but that was still fifty miles away. It was just about ticking boxes I thought, just work on one box at a time. What do I need to get through this? Food, water, more clothes! I was in a small village so no chance of buying some clothes, but there should be somewhere for warm food and a coffee. If I could just feel some sort of comfort I could get through another night, and I could then get everything I needed from my drop bag. It was a plan; even if a few details were missing, it was still a plan. I'm not lying though; I was definitely nervous about another Moor crossing through the night with the little clothing I had available. As I was searching through Google maps to see what shops were close by, an old VW transporter pulled up next to me. The window juddered down as a big hairy man, who had obviously spent some time in the wilds, manually wound it down and stuck his head out. "Hey Stuart, I'm part of the race support, how are you doing? We've been watching you on the GPS for the last few hours to make sure you're ok". He continued with, "You do realise you shouldn't have left the tent, and this is the first opportunity we've had to see you, so let's just have a quick look at ya". He then repeated the same thing I heard in the tent, "Staying hyperthermic and feeling hyperthermia for as long as you did can be a little dangerous, and it can come back to bite you in the ass at any time in the next day or so". Whilst he was explaining this, he removed my gloves and went "Mmm" and then removed my shoes and socks.

Immediately he said, "That's it, my friend, you are out". "What do you mean, out? "It's game over for you son, you've gone hyperthermic again. You've got no return in your hands and your feet are blue. I'm sorry, but I'm not allowing you to head back out to do twenty plus miles of moorland in this condition". He concerningly continued, "It would be very difficult to get you back down when things go tits up for ya".

That was it! Done! Finished! Caput! Shit, shit, shit, shit! Another DNF, another race where I did everything right when preparing, only to be kicked in the balls by an accident and bad luck. Another waste of money and a waste of bloody time.

It wasn't a very pleasant journey home. My emotions were bubbling. I was pissed off and I didn't really say much to anyone. I must have shown a very disturbed energy because people would start to talk to me and then stop mid-sentence before realising this wasn't the time or the person for chit chat. I had to wait for an hour to get collected from my location before waiting another hour or so for my drop bag to arrive at the checkpoint where I was sulking. Then a kind lady took a few of us non-finishers to the nearest train station to figure out our journeys home. All of this time was spent with a hood over my head and earphones in my ears. There was nothing playing on them, I was just using them to let others believe there was so that nobody would attempt to talk to me. All I could think about was my bad luck and misfortunes during all my big races recently. Two more attempts at the 6633 Arctic Ultra. The first one took three years to actually get my feet on Canadian soil because of Covid, and then it wasn't even an official race route, so it didn't really count for anything. The second attempt happened to be held during the worst storm in the race's history, destroying the route and forcing an alternative one, which also wasn't classified as an official race attempt. Added to this, I've had to come to terms with the fact I received the incorrect information from race officials resulting in another 'did not finish'. Then came the UTS100 where someone turned the oven up to scorchio for just two days when I'd been training in the wettest and windiest winter and spring we'd seen in years, forcing the biggest drop-out percentage in the history of the race. And now the Summer Spine race, which took place at the end of a relentless few months of rain, creating even worse running conditions than what would be expected during the winter one, also making this year's race achieve the biggest DNF rate in its history.

I was beginning to lose my love for the game. No, I'll rephrase that. I was starting to hate it because the love went away a long time ago.

Chapter 8

Metamorphosis

When Teri prematurely collected me from the train station, after another failed attempt at a high-end adventurous race, the energy coming from both of us wasn't comfortable. My persistent need to participate in these ridiculous challenges, along with the addiction to the training and the single-mindedness to achieve my goals, was tiresome to everyone around me, but mostly Teri. I knew that, in recent times, my activities and my uninterrupted drive to be at the peak of my capabilities had isolated me from my loved ones. In fact, most people I connected with through work, friendship, love or blood, unfortunately ended up receiving a lesser version of me than they deserved. I could never relax, I could never let go of the upcoming challenge, even for just a minute, allowing myself to feel anything other than the drive. No other emotions had a chance at the driving seat because I was so scared I wouldn't find the focus again. Reassessing my behaviour, I believed that even my work was suffering as clients started drifting away. I would constantly talk to them about the misfortunes of my last event, and how I was planning to learn from them in preparation for the next venture. I was drained, and I was draining my family as they repeatedly dropped hints and had little stabs at me about how I was never there. Even if my body was present, my mind would be calculating and assessing choices I had made on strategies, or equipment, or trying to balance my diary for the next day so I could achieve the required amount of training. I hadn't really viewed a whole movie with the family for years or truly been a constructive part of a discussion. I'm guessing clients were drained too, which showed in the reducing number of classes I was teaching, and the lack of communication from friends for a pint, or a coffee for a chat.

Although the drive home was only thirty minutes, it felt a lot longer than that. We sat mostly in silence, both of us fully aware that we wanted, and needed, the relentless cycle that I was trapped in, to stop. Both of us knew that whatever I said would fall on deaf ears because I would have said it dozens of times before. I couldn't count the number of times I'd said I wasn't going to do it anymore; how many times I'd said I hate this game, and I was done with it; and then how many times I'd found a backdoor into the addictive part of my mind to allow me to have one more go. I would convince myself I just needed a little taste, a little hit to make the separation from my addiction somewhat more comfortable. Knowing that, once I was allowed to step through the back door, the games were afoot again, and I would have the power to slowly build the intensity of the fix. There were no words I could say to Teri, no verbal diarrhoea that would carry any weight. I could see that she didn't want to hear any reasons or excuses as to why I was home early with my tail between my legs - again.

There was something different this time though. I'm sure I've said that before too, but there was. I wasn't just angry at another DNF; I hated the game and everything that was connected to it. If the game was something I could physically hold and hurt, I would. I'd have my hands around its neck, squeezing as hard as

I could, screaming with hysterical tears in my eyes until it stopped twitching, and then I would bring the fucking thing back to life just so I could frantically and deliriously enjoy the whole process again. I loathed it and detested who I'd become as a consequence of it. I knew, in my heart, I had washed my hands of it, but Teri would have rolled her eyes and said, 'Whatever you say baby' as she'd turn away to get busy doing something more interesting, like washing up or watching the grass grow. It was a pointless exercise to try and communicate this discovery.

Entering the house and still with no interaction with Teri, I released this tension and anger by moving all my medals and trophies into the loft, placing whatever I had of value that had anything to do with the running world up for sale, and everything else I wouldn't need for general exercise in the bin. Most of my books went into a box and were stored away, and I deleted 'Audible' off my phone, so I didn't have to read or listen to any more bullshit about pushing your limits, living at the edge of your comfort zone, or getting back up on your feet when life has beat the shit out of you. I even deleted most of my internet friends who were into running. I didn't want to see it, hear about it, be around it or have anything to do with anyone who was in any shape or form connected with it. I was done; it had beaten me. It had taken everything I was willing to give it, and that was a lot, as I'd given a huge chunk of my life to it. I wasn't asking for much in return. All I wanted was one grand finale to celebrate my ten-plus years of dedication and loyalty to the relationship. Just one big, hands in the air, teary-eyed, confetti-as-rain, I fucking did it, moment. But no, that just happens in the bloody movies.

At the beginning of this journey, I believed the unfinished adventures and challenges were my doing, my fault. I hadn't trained well enough; I had bought the wrong type and cheapest equipment I could find; I had the wrong mindset. Then, a few years ago, I believe I switched on to what this sport requires to be successful, and accepted I needed to give it more. I realised the commitment to the relationship needed to be raised, so my game stepped up. I trained without fear, emotion or consequence. I selfishly spent exactly what needed to be spent, without question. I was mentally invested, researching everything I possibly could, to the sacrifice of everyone and everything else around me in the hope I could just have that romantic Disney finish to this chapter of my life. I so wanted to have that poetic end I thought I needed to say goodbye to this world and walk away towards the dusky sunset as my silhouette shimmered from the rising heat evaporating from the earth.

It turns out I was still wrong; I was the same as I always was - delusional. The effort and engagement I gave to the sport increased my odds of success slightly, but only slightly. I now understand that in this ultra-athletic world, what you do, how you prepare and how you approach an event is only a small percentage of your success. It's mostly luck. It's just luck. It's luck that determines the weather, it's luck at how other people's influences affect your progress, and it's just luck if you manage to not slip, get hyperthermia, break a leg or get sent the wrong way. I found that participating in events with a distance up to, say, a marathon, is mostly to do with your preparation and research. But the further you go into the ultra-running world, the further it swings to the hand you have been dealt at the table on that specific day. I understand the need to train in preparation for all situations and consequences, but the more stones that are thrown at you, the higher chance of being hit, and I was completely pissed off with being hit. I was done with it. I was done with sacrificing my weekends, time with my family, losing sleep, spending unnecessary money, and living in this hole I was spending hours and hours a week trying to run out of.

A few weeks later, and I was still feeling partly euphoric about becoming strong enough to walk away from my chains and partly feeling empty because I had no chains to keep me company. It was time to fulfil a promise to an old friend, Sylvia. In 2020, the year Covid struck if you ever needed a reminder, I was supposed to guide Sylvia and her family around Chamonix in the French Alps. This had been on the cards for a few years, but we never found the time, eventually booking it for the summer of 2020. We all know what happened that summer, so it sat on the shelf for a few more years until 2024 when things had settled down. I'd escaped the ties of my gym, and all of Sylvia's family were in a position to travel at the same time, so it was time to fulfil a seven-year promise.

Chamonix has always been and will always be a special place for me. I've spent an uncountable number of weekends, and an immeasurable number of miles, hiking various paths throughout that valley. I have taken various people of all physical capabilities over the past twelve years on incredible adventures, so they could see how far they could be pushed. Every visit was different, different challenges, different routes, different people and different energies. The one thing that was constant was the thinking time. It's a place to grow, accept, rebalance, plan, and understand who and where you are with yourself. Standing in Chamonix at the foot of Mont Blanc, feeling its dominance whilst it provocatively stares down at you from its heavenly four-and-a-half-kilometre height, it silently talks to you. It likes to remind you how insignificant you are and how irrelevant your problems are. It loves explaining how it's been standing there for fifteen million years and seen lots of comings and goings during that time; many earthly phases, climate changes, populations and species. It's seen things in the heavens we can only imagine, and storms passing through that could destroy anything in its way. In fact, the last really big freeze lasted one hundred thousand years when Mont Blanc never saw anything but snow in any direction during that time. The global issues that mountain has witnessed is unfathomable. So, when you've stared hard enough and for long enough at its wise and seductive white peak, you'll see it give a little wink as it humbles you into submission with its history. This, then, allows you to feel free from the unrelenting burdens life asks you to carry through your journey. Even if just for a moment. It's this freedom from life's pressures that provides a safe passage to think openly about yourself and strangely encourages the blocked doorways to happily widen so you can see alternative options, or the different pathways that are available in front of you.

This most recent adventure did not disappoint. Every visit to Chamonix, regardless of the company I've enjoyed, I find there's always a period when I'm on my own. This allows me to open my eyes for the first time in months, and to start to experience these doors opening. I feel the freedom and the timeless energy wave over me as my future widens and my peripheral vision goes into overdrive, absorbing and processing more sensory data than any supercomputer could possibly handle. This happened on the last day of this adventure at a very beautiful and majestic place called Lac Blanc.

This is my favourite location in my favourite place, with a view that causes you to temporarily stop breathing. It's a small lake 1,500 metres above the valley, with a small refuge that sits next to its crystal blue water. The picture postcard view is finished with the snow creeping down the mountain peaks which cap three sides of the lake. The fourth side exposes the view of dreams where you can see the whole valley and miles of aggressive, rocky summits well into Italy and Switzerland. During the busiest part of the hiking season, you can grab a slice of homemade blueberry tart and a strong, but expensive coffee from this refuge, just to polish off the occasion. After some time adoring its splendour, Sylvia and her crew descended back down the valley, dribbling at the thought of more coffee and pastries from the cafe at the top of the cable car lift, some 500 meters below. This left me to have some quality time to myself; time to absorb the energy from the Mont Blanc massif mountain range laid out in front of me, sculpted and painted by my favourite artist, mother nature. The view is vast and endless, but at the same time so enveloping you could almost reach out and hug it.

This place is special for me and my family. This was the 'Everest' my wife believed had signified her return to fitness and health. We had passed through Chamonix as part of an Italian driving holiday to celebrate our 10th wedding anniversary. It was in 2016, about fifteen months after we drastically changed how we lived our lives to become healthier and fitter. This holistic shift resulted in a dramatic change in both of us, but mostly for Teri. Two years before our stopover in Chamonix, my wife had spent most of her days in a wheelchair, unable to climb stairs without succumbing to using her bum to travel between floors. On a really bad day, she couldn't even take care of herself. Basically, her life had stopped as she was no longer able to manage as a functional person. But on that day, in July 2016, in this special place as we celebrated our 10th wedding anniversary, she climbed nearly 1,500 metres covering sixteen miles without help or support. It was a very memorable day and gave us a special location to put a flag in the sand, for both of us. The greatest respect needs to be given to both my daughters as well, as they were only ten and thirteen years old at the time and didn't moan at all as they were in awe of seeing their mum climb up that mountain. Still today, that experience goes down as one of my top ten favourite days.

When we all reached the top, in the middle of the afternoon on that day, the mercury touched 30 degree Celsius. It was a glorious day until, almost instantly, the sunshine gave way to a huge, dark, menacing cloud that travelled down the sides of the mountains to surround us. All of a sudden, we were inside a very intimidating darkness, unable to see ten meters in any direction. Within minutes, frightening clashes of thunder shook the ground, and forks of lightning flashed in the gloom. The rain was almost painful as it created small craters in the sandy mud next to our feet. Everyone scampered into the small refuge like meerkats running from an eagle. The refuge was a basic building with stone walls, concrete floors and a couple of wooden benches thrown together with some leftover wood. There was a small kitchen with simple cooking utensils, allowing the possibility to make hot drinks and a few snacks. At the end of a hallway were a couple of cold, stoney-walled toilets. Once we had assessed our new dwelling, we lifted our heads to see that there were a couple of dozen people, standing there in disbelief. They were all staring out the windows at the power of this storm, wondering in silence if it would ease enough so they could get back down to civilization that evening. We all knew it was at least a three-hour hard trek back down, and that would mean arriving at dusk if we left right now. It wasn't long before we came to terms with the fact we would be spending the night on this hard floor, as we didn't have the equipment for a night hike and would run the risk of getting lost without a torch. Just as we were planning the best place in the room to settle down and try to get some sort of comfort for the night ahead, there was a break in the rain, and the sky brightened slightly. It was now or never we thought, gambling that the storm had moved on and was finished with us. Quick as a flash we were dressed in our waterproofs, rucksacks on our backs, and marching down the mountain with intent. Unfortunately, when we were just far enough away from the refuge, we lost the gamble. The heavens opened again, releasing another powerful downpour along with biblical thunder and lightning. This joined us on our journey for the entirety of our descent into the valley. It was scaringly exciting, even for me, but I can't imagine how the girls were feeling. After an hour or so we could see the lights of Chamonix below us. We were soaked to the skin, shivering uncontrollably, and the full darkness of the night had joined us: but even though we had empty bellies and felt very dehydrated we all sang and danced our way down the last few miles. We were totally caught up in the absurdity of the situation, feeling as energised and enthusiastic as pigs in shit. We had never felt, before or since, so exhilarated and totally connected with our environment and each other. We didn't have a care in the world as we paraded side by side through the streets of Chamonix, splashing and dancing past a cascade of onlookers who were suited and booted for their evenings out. It was amazing and still stands as one of the best days we've spent together.

Backtracking to my long-awaited, and much needed secluded moment at Lac Blanc, as I placed myself at the end of a huge rock, with the valley a mile below me and the mountain range stretching out a couple of miles above me, I could feel the locked doors of other possibilities opening, as they always do here. As usual, the answer I was hoping to receive started to materialise in front of me, much like the yellow brick road in The Wizard of Oz.

The answer was simple really. It hit me like a slap around the face from a kipper and continued to hit me. Slap, 'I'm too old for this shit'. Another slap, 'I'm too old for this shit', and another, but louder, 'I'M TOO OLD FOR THIS SHIIIIT'. I'm too old to do things I don't want to do anymore, and I'm too old to be around people I don't want to be around, and I'm especially too old for any more bullshit, specifically from myself. It felt like the valley spoke to me. I'd lived most of my life afraid of upsetting people at my expense, doing things to please others whilst sacrificing my own needs; listening to everyone else's issues as they showed no regard to mine; going places I didn't want to go; being with people I didn't want to be with, and basically living a life that constantly used me. No part of my life was mine, and to hide this, to put a band aid over this relentlessly bleeding cut, I ran, took drugs, drank alcohol, smoked cigarettes, ate crap, gambled and anything else I could escape into. I would do things that gave me a few seconds or minutes or even hours of selfish isolation. Sometimes to indulge in silence, sometimes to rebel against the cage I felt around me, and sometimes to feel the pain, my pain, the pain that would make me feel I still had at least one emotion left of my own.

For the first fifty years of my life this pain became a friend I needed to visit every now and then. I ran until I felt it, I'd sabotage joyful moments to reconnect with it, I'd stay awake all night to enjoy its company the next day, and I'd start arguments with loved ones or sell things I really wanted to keep just to keep it walking alongside me. I now realise this wasn't a masochistic act; this was because, occasionally, I needed to feel something, anything that was mine.

My life was spent looking out for others, lifting, carrying, supporting and caring for everyone else. Whenever anyone felt discomfort, I was there with advice, an ear, a muscle or a hug. I'm not trying to sell myself as some sort of angel, because I'm not. A lot of the time I resented the situation and myself for getting involved, for taking on more burdens and giving myself more of a load to carry. I'm an angry person most of the time. There are times I just wanted to tell whoever it is to sort out their own shit, but I couldn't. I wanted to say I had plenty of my own to shovel. I resented myself for it and anger began to build. I repressed this anger through pain. It seems that it was the only way I could feel myself anymore. I just kept going around in circles while anger was building. A painful release was then needed, and once it was felt, a temporary calmness flowed before the anger built once again. Other emotions couldn't seem to break the routine, and I didn't feel much else beyond this.

I'm no psychiatrist but, analysing my past, I suppose it started when I was maybe four or five years old when

I used to go downstairs and cuddle with my mum after she'd had an argument with dad, and she was left crying after he'd stormed out with a slam of the door. Then, when the divorce came, and being the eldest, I'd comfort my brother and sister. I grew up quickly. Life was tough for our mum at that time. Trying to hold down two jobs to look after three children became impossible, so she was forced to send us to live with our dad and a very resentful stepmother. Our dad was constantly at work or out with his football mates, which left the resentful stepmom to supposedly care for us. In other words, I became the carer and the shoulder to cry on more so than ever for my siblings. I felt the parental role fall on my shoulders. Years later I paved the way for us to run away from this cold home and reunite with our mum, now that she had managed to somewhat get back on her feet, although she still needed to work two jobs to maintain it. I was thirteen now and a better age to look after the three of us until mum would return from work. I think this is when I began emotionally disconnecting and subconsciously built walls to prevent me from slowing down. I had a lot to hold up and didn't have time to think about it.

Once life had moved on and we all became adults, I'm guessing I lived in my addictions to give myself a burden, something to carry on my back so I could still feel something, anything. I found connecting with anyone or anything quite difficult, and living with a weight to carry was the easiest way to connect with something. In every career I've had, I quickly moved up to management, not because I'm career oriented, but because I need to carry a burden; I need to feel the pressure. I feel comfort in discomfort. I knew as a manager I could help, support and carry my team.

The first twelve to fourteen years of my relationship with Teri was like throwing petrol on the cinders of my dwindling emotional bank, reigniting the life into my burden-carrying back, squashing down anything else I might want or need to feel for myself. Working sixty hours a week, taking care of a wife who became disabled while raising two daughters, and staying on top of the household duties such as cooking, cleaning, shopping, walking dogs, paying bills and keeping up with home repairs, was enough to close me down emotionally. The walls were high and impenetrable, and I became a master at pretending everything was ok. So much so that I believe it's the reason I've been so successful as a Health Coach. My tolerance for emotional pain is unwavering, and my acting ability to pretend everything is going to be ok is so convincing that I can empathise, absorb, connect, and improve my clients' state of mind, time after time, hour after hour and day after day. I have been coaching for ten years now, which equates to over 15,000 sessions of listening to people's problems, empathising with their stories, giving my advice or opinions, or even honesty if I feel they can take it, and a hell of a lot of hugs. I can honestly count on one hand the number of times they have left my studio feeling worse than when they walked in.

Being a shoulder to cry on and having a back that's strong enough to carry so many people for so long, has enforced an emotional switch-off and made me feel connected to despair, pain, heartache and discomfort. Anger would build, pain released it, comfort temporarily came, and then I would start again.

Time had become my adversary. Having spare time in the day was dangerous. Space to think hurt; space allowed me to connect with my anger, which needed a quick fix. I had spent so many of my days being consumed with other people's problems that I had had no time to keep my emotional balance in order. If the unfortunate thing happened and I found myself with a few minutes to sit and contemplate, I would find a shovel and start digging, find a way to stay completely submerged so the onslaught of unrecognisable emotions couldn't find me. Happy times were difficult to navigate; they were uncontrollable and difficult to act out. A certain level of anguish had to be injected into the occasion to make them palatable. At parties I would make sure I spent the entire time cleaning up after people, fetching drinks, cooking, being a gofer, and finding the closest person who looked like they needed emotional support. On holidays I would be slightly on edge all the time, creating enough tension in the camp to force discomfort and maybe the odd argument; just to release the pressure. My birthday - bloody hell - the worst day of the year. There was no escape on that day.

Being emotionally aware of yourself is something that needs to be exercised daily, just like any other muscle. The lack of use will make the connection weak and unusable, thus creating a lack of connection with others, or places and situations. You may look like you have sympathy and empathy, laughter and joyfulness, anger and aggression, appreciation and connection, even passion and excitement, but it's just an improved acting ability built from the university of life. As another emotion switches off, the ability to act through it improves.

Sitting on that rock above that valley with that view, and in that moment, all this was shown to me in a few seconds. My answer was 'NO MORE'. No more doing stuff I didn't want to do; no more being with people I didn't want to be with; no more listening to shit I didn't want to listen to, especially at the sacrifice of putting me first. As mentioned before, my world is the three ladies I devote my life to, and if I am going to enjoy, and be emotionally part of their future, I have to start this reconnection with myself. I wasn't actually sure what that meant or what it was going to feel like, but the ball had to start rolling down the hill. I hit my fifties a year ago, which meant I probably had more time behind me than in front; quite a sobering thought, but the slap around the face I needed to start this metamorphosis straight away.

Rising from the rock, and voicing thanks with my hands clenched together and a little bow towards the valley for its guidance once again, I made my way back down to the others in deep thought, trying to understand what it meant to put myself first. How do I practise that; what are the stepping stones to achieving it; what are the rules; and more importantly, would I be able to reconnect with the few emotions that had not been out to play for a long time? Less than an hour later I reached the top of the cable lift at a place called La Flegere. This is where we would descend back into the valley, and the others were waiting for my arrival and showing some anxiousness to complete the journey back to our accommodation. I was lost in my own space and felt so embedded in the thoughts that were growing that I didn't really engage with the rest of the team. I yearned for more time alone, so separated from them at the bottom of the cable lift to once again walk on my own back to town whilst they all jumped on a bus, agreeing to meet me at a restaurant later on. I was honestly feeling quite anxious and uncomfortable to be around others, so headed off on my own in the direction of Chamonix centre along a fast, rumbling, powerful river. But that didn't really matter as I could have been walking anywhere. I took in none of my surroundings. I felt nothing from the beauty of my environment, and I didn't even want to be in Chamonix anymore. I just wanted to be with my family and to share my revelations with them. Thankfully, the flight home was the next day, which meant I only had to be sociable for another twenty-four hours. But, in that, lies the whole problem, doesn't it? Why should I put on an act? I thought this was a turning point; this is the point I would start relaxing into my own emotions and let them happen instead of burying them, squashing them down, hiding them until they refuse to come out. I knew I didn't want to be here anymore, so why pretend? The next twenty-four hours were spent planning and processing, writing, reading and listening, trying to find a way forward. Preparing a plan to provide a safe passage away from my addictions and the freedom to explore myself a bit. The goal, to find my emotions, to start looking forward to things, anything, and to feel excitement about doing activities for myself. To feel pleasure in sunsets, and the joy in life's gifts, but most of all, to find my 'passion'. I talk a lot about passion, especially in my first book. It's a massive word for me and something I try to instil in as many people as I can. It doesn't matter what you are passionate about, just as long as you feel it. Passion is what should drive us, not wealth or possessions. These are dense veils placed over our souls to prevent us from being driven by things that might actually awaken our minds and create free thinking. Free thinkers are dangerous; they move in unconventional ways. They are unpredictable and cherish life itself, not the objects within it. In my mind, passion is where life exists, where it begins and where it ends. It's excitement, adrenaline, youthfulness and love. It's the foundation that's built this world around us, its cities and buildings, churches, schools, planes, cars and bridges. It's our whole existence. Unfortunately, as much as I have been talking about it and explaining it in many of my stories, I haven't felt it for some time. The closest I get to it is that I am passionate in the pursuit of passion.

One realisation that came to me on the journey home was that I didn't want to race anymore. Not,' I'm going to stop because I know I should', but I *really* didn't want to race anymore. I now understood that this had become the next negative addiction in a long chain of negative addictions, and taking as much away from me and my family as any other addiction I'd had. Accepting this for the first time reduced the weight from my shoulders, removed the pressure instantly from the expectations I had put on myself, and from what others, I assumed, expected from me. I felt free for the first time. The shackles had gone. Free from the years of safety blankets that I had hidden behind. Safety blankets that had protected and distracted me from getting to know myself. Worryingly, this meant that like it or not, I was inevitably going to have to face the mirror and have some alone time. Shit, I thought, this could hurt.

It did hurt! The first week or two were cool as I proudly floated through the honeymoon period, explaining to everyone how excited I was about moving on and escaping the shackles. But it wasn't long before a new weight burdened me. There was empty space, room for thought and time to look at myself. I was a complete mess, jumping from one emotion to another, fighting for continuity. I was a hormonal teenager again, sometimes up, sometimes down. I was happy, depressed, bouncy, angry and repressed, switching moods mid-sentence, and confusing everyone around me. My family must have been treading on eggshells. I would lose direction and miss appointments. I'd get angry at Disney movies and cry at horror films. I got completely pissed off because I had no clue as to why I had walked into the kitchen and couldn't remember why I was there. I could find myself standing in the middle of the supermarket with no idea what I was supposed to be doing, or even if that was the reason I left the house, feeling totally confused and holding back the tears. Time after time I would leave the house to do something important, only to return feeling like I'd buggered up and forgotten to do something I had promised to do. For three months, for the whole of July, August and September, I would have been perfectly happy not to have woken up the next day; and not just the next day, but ever. If it was game over for me, then so be it; I'd be at peace as I was tired of fighting. I had accepted defeat and life had beaten me. I conceded. I wanted to get off this bloody train. I just wanted someone to take me away from this torment.

I tried to fill the gaps, throwing myself into things I knew would pass the time and make me feel a little joy. I started writing again, it's in those three months that I wrote most of this book. I joined the local gym to get out of the house and hopefully meet some people who didn't require anything from me. I even bought a second-hand guitar and dedicated thirty minutes to it every day. My motorbike started coming out of the garage more than once a month, and my beloved husky-cross dog 'Sheba' was getting extra walks. Every day it was easier to squeeze in some of these activities, with time to spare. I began to realise how much of my days had been spent devoted to my addiction.

It's now November and it's working. I'm feeling other stuff, I'm feeling excited some mornings about going to the gym, not just for the exercise but to have a chat. One of the first things I do is plan when I can get thirty minutes of the day to pick up the guitar. I can even throw a few tunes together now without making the dog howl. Work is becoming easier, and I am feeling more relaxed about letting things go if I can't manage them that day. I think I'm starting to prioritise myself a little bit. I've promised myself two hours a day to do what makes me feel - well, feelings. Two hours that I refuse to give up even if I have to decline work or not do something for someone else or clean the house. Everything else will just have to wait. Two hours a day when I just say no, this is my time.

I know there will be highs and lows, and periods of slipping into shit again, but that's just life. I'm feeling ready to take on the next chapter. The girls have grown into amazingly confident people, still with a lot to learn as we all do, but they are flying themselves now. Teri has her own life and is finding her own balance, and I'm content with how I make money. It does sometimes become heavy, but I've got some healthier, more relaxing releases now, and it enables me to have a certain level of freedom each day. Financially, we can pay the bills each month and the house look like a home. It's time to enjoy some time with Teri doing the stuff we have been promising ourselves for twenty-five years. It's time to move into another 'lifetime' within our lifetime.

Lifetimes within a lifetime!

A useful concept I talk about with my daughters is my belief we start a new life within our lifetime around every seven to eight years. It can be quite painful during the transition from one lifetime to another. Change is always painful, usually made worse by the refusal to accept it. Staying comfortable is what we strive to achieve, but being comfortable is, in my eyes, a dangerous place. Fighting to stay in the comfort zone actually creates the pain. Think about receiving an injection. If you tense the muscle instead of relaxing and accepting the discomfort, it hurts more. Like it or not though, these changing lifetimes happen, and we don't have a choice. We can try and fight it, holding onto the life we currently have, but you know something doesn't feel right and something has to change. The inevitable will happen, and the change will come.

All of a sudden, after seven years or so, the relationship suffers a blip, and arguments start developing because each one wants something different from life now. Maybe you suddenly feel you are going nowhere in your work and need a change to feel recognised. You might feel the urge to move house for a quieter lifestyle or a busier one. Starting a family might jump up the priority ladder all of a sudden. These are all driven by hormonal changes creating a different outlook on life and different needs. The biggest lifetime switch is around fourteen years old, and we all know what a car crash that change feels like. This is what I spoke about with my daughters when they played Jekyll and Hyde for three years, explaining that this is the transition from lifetime number two into lifetime number three. It's going to happen, and it will be a rough ride, but rolling with it will make the storm pass slightly easier than trying to fight against it. Just understanding the fact that it's just a switch from one lifetime into another usually helps.

This is how I have personally felt my life change every few years, creating lifetimes within my lifetime. I've also seen these changes happen in many other people of all ages around me. Look back at your life to see if you have felt something similar:

From birth to seven years old you are still growing and developing, but obviously now out in the wide world and no longer in the womb.

Between ages seven to fourteen you become self-aware as you try to get a grasp on the world and what it feels like. You feel some new emotions for the first time as they try to find some continuity.

Fourteen to twenty-one. The shit show happens as mother nature decides to really throw a spanner in the works and give you an unfiltered amount of the new hormones that change you from wanting to play with toys to wanting to play with other people, if you know what I mean. These lovely little hormones that have been slowly building up, giggling to themselves because they know what's coming. They have been plotting against you, knowing they are about to take you to a four-year long party of crying, laughing, screaming, punching, anger and depression, every single day. Then, as the party quietens down, you go looking under all the rocks and in nightclubs for all the other hormonal 'carrier monkeys' trying to find someone who is as equally screwed up as you are, in the hope you could possibly couple up and create a future.

Twenty-one to twenty-eight: you've found your equally-messed-up match and go in search of a nest, eagerly looking in various places for the best location to raise some offspring. Working hard, collecting branches and twigs to make it as safe as possible.

Twenty-eight to thirty-five: yay, is it blue or pink balloons? Little creatures arrive. Your parenting hormones wake up. Your own life doesn't matter anymore. Every waking moment is distracted by small humans who haven't finished developing yet, and who need total sacrifice from you and your relationships with everything and everyone. You find yourself crying and screaming into bottles of gin, 'WHEN WILL IT EVER END?'.

Thirty-five to forty-two: this is a brief reprieve from the chaos. Your children become a little more independent, and you have managed to move up the ladder a bit at work. Money has hopefully become a little less of a problem, and you can start venturing out again as you actually feel like a grown up for the first time. Even the hormones are less reactive and are calming down, which you take as a gift initially, but you have no idea what's coming. Unfortunately, this calmness has a downside. Your body has started misbehaving; it's started moaning about a few things, and relishes quiet time rather than party time. It's relaxing you into middle age and preparing you for the down turn.

Here it is; woohoo! middle age - forty-two to forty-nine. The weight of life starts sitting on your shoulders. Unusual tiredness keeps you awake at night, and you walk every morning like you have been riding a horse for three hours the day before, until, that is, you've injected caffeine into the system.

Midlife crisis time comes between forty-nine to fifty-six. Hormones have taken a nosedive as your body says, it doesn't need you anymore. It's time to just sit there and wait for the last page. That's what it feels like anyway. Kids don't need you anymore, apart from being a taxi and a bank. In fact, it's not that they don't need you, they actually resent you for embarrassing them by your presence as you cling onto them for dear life trying to keep a foot hold onto any form of youthfulness you can find. As I sit here typing these words, slap bang in the middle of this lifecycle, I can say that this is the hardest cycle outside the teenage years, for me anyway. It's the loneliest I've felt. Kids have flown away, the lack of hormones have taken away purpose, and for the first time you have to find out who you are as an adult without parenting, reduced drive, needs and ambition. It's time for reinvention. If you don't accept this change, it'll bite you in the arse. It's actually time to use the heart as a driving force and not the hormones. What do you like and dislike; what hobbies do you have and interests you wished you had time for. Maybe learn an instrument or a language; travel and meet new people, join some clubs, renovate a car or some furniture, take up carpentry. This could become the best life of all your lives. It's like life 2.0 has begun. Without the hormones to feed ego and sexual drive, nesting or protection, you have to learn to do things because you want to and not should do. It's tough but roll with it and you could create some freedom.

Fifty-six onwards. Hormonally, everything is quiet and calmed down. You have reached the last lifetime within a lifetime. The negative and hard thing is that you are slowly deteriorating. There is nothing to drive the need for good looks or muscle or athleticism; nothing to drive ambition or progress, and nothing to keep you awake at night, which is frustrating because you can't sleep anymore. But, on the positive side, you have learned who you are and what you want. If you have played your hand right by working hard and looking after your own and your family's health and wealth, you can look at what you have achieved with great satisfaction. You can reminisce on how you've developed a lovely family and been part of some lasting relationships, built wealth and memories, experienced love and interactions, and now, with fifty-six plus years of building your foundations you have enough finances, health and a carefree attitude to spend the rest of your years doing 'you'. You have done your bit for biology and worked hard enough to be able to slow down and feel life rather than be uncontrollably pushed through it. Depression, which often results from the past, has possibly lifted as you no longer give a shit about it. Stress has subsided because you have hopefully learnt to live life one step, one second and one breath at a time. Anxiety has taken a back seat because you've accepted that tomorrow is a gift, and experiencing another day in whatever shape or form it comes in, is good enough.

While writing this chapter of the book, I did a little research into this concept and found that a philosopher called Rudolf Steiner first wrote and spoke about this very thing in the 20th century. He wrote many books around the belief of the seven-year periods of life, and how they are bigger than just a guide through our lifetime. He talks about re-birth and planetary spheres; a theory that vastly expands our miniscule existences. Very fascinating literature, and definitely worth some time if it's of interest to you.

Strangely, this coincides with the biological understanding that our bodies complete a whole physical transformation over a seven-year period. Cells renew at different speeds, skin recycles every two weeks, heart cells are renewed every nine months, and stomach and intestinal cells only last around five days before being replaced, but the longest living cells are the bones which are regenerated over seven to eight years. Basically, everything in the mirror, apart from your eyes and teeth, are no more than around seven years old. This is a constantly flowing activity that happens at a rate of approximately eight hundred thousand new cells every second of our life. That shocks me every time I say it. We are constantly changing and adapting to the world and the universe as we pass through it, mentally, physically and hormonally. These changes happen regardless. We have no control over it and are mostly unaware, spending a large percentage of our lives fighting against a system that most of us don't even know exists. It's inevitable and relentless and will be very painful if you refuse to move with it. Flowing with it, understanding it's happening and then being guided by it, makes for a much more pleasurable and connected experience. I wish I had felt this before fighting against the natural universal rhythm of existence for the first years of my life. I guess that's the beauty and the wisdom of ageing.

Chapter 9

Get it right first time!

When all is said and done, the journey continues regardless of your interference, planning or guidance. From day one to day zero you can only do what you can with the knowledge you have at that time. You can wish and hope for the best outcome, but subconsciously you need to always prepare for the worst. Just when you feel you have it all figured out, life sends you on a tangent to confuse the shit out of everything, all over again, reminding you that control is an illusion. All you can do is be true to yourself and your loved ones, and remind yourself every day that this is it, this is all there is, in regard to your time on this rock. If you don't get it right the first time .... tough. This is all you have.

I am only fifty-one years old, with hopefully a few decades of life left to experience, but I do have fifty-one very full years of experience. I've passed through a scary amount of shit times, but equally, danced along merrily in the sunshine of many joyous, happy and uplifting times. I've been in the gutter and been on top of the world. I've felt true love, and I've felt heartache. I've hated myself and had times of loving myself. I've experienced bankruptcy and had times when I've had a few notes in my pocket. There have been times when I've pushed myself harder than most people only dare to dream about or even have nightmares about. There have been weeks at a time when I've been in the pits of drug and alcohol abuse and also experienced the discipline and determination to stay away from alcohol for ten years, exactly to the day, before celebrating with a pint with my family. I've experienced a family break up as a child and an adult but have been part of my own new world of three amazing people, and soon, to feel part of my daughters' growing worlds. I've had times when I wanted life to end and times when I wanted to live forever. I've lived so many lifetimes already and still feel life has only just begun.

Putting pen to paper, or fingers to keys, over the past few years as I've passed on stories and experiences to whoever wants to read them, has been a journey in itself. A journey that has made me look hard at myself and the world around me as I reminisce about my failures and successes, joys and depressions, growths and declines, and loves and losses. I've sat here for hours, day after day, contemplating my journey so far and looking for answers, reasons why, and maybe some lessons hidden in the debris and dust that has been left in its wake. Hopefully, I have absorbed a few things that could be useful to others. So, if it was at all possible, what lessons of life would I pass on to my younger self? What words of wisdom can I enlighten my future generations with, along with anyone else that isn't tired of listening to me babble on, or the babbling of everyone else throughout the social-inter-webinnal world. After all, I think we are all getting a little fed up with the amount of unqualified, unsanctioned advice on screens. Everyone these days seems to have a say, an opinion and a perception of what it takes to be happy, healthy, wealthy, fulfilled and wise.

So, here's mine. Here are a few of my particular lessons I try to live by: a few phrases or quotes that have left a mark on me, in me, or even become part of me. They are not in any order of relevance or importance; I just pull on them when I need them. They guide me when I need guiding, kick me when I need kicking, lift me when I need lifting, and remind me when I forget what an arsehole or an idiot I'm being.

1. **When you want to be successful as much as you want to breathe, then you will be successful!**

This is a quote I heard from a guy called Eric Thomas. Eric Thomas grew up in Chicago the hard way, spending a lot of his teenage years living on the streets. He really does know what it's like to hit the bottom at an early age and then find the tenacity to build himself up one decision and one brick at a time. He has become one of the most respected and influential motivational speakers in the world, and has created a wealth of knowledge, finances and life lessons that he enthusiastically shares with everyone that he comes in contact with. I get goosebumps every time I hear this guy talk and I feel motivated to do whatever it takes to achieve whatever it is I am fighting for.

The story goes: there was this young man who wanted to make a lot of money, so he went to his guru and said to the guru, “I want to be on the same financial level as you. Can you teach me? " The guru replied, “If you want to be on the same level as I am on then meet me on the beach tomorrow morning at 4am”. “At the beach?” the young guy questions, “ I want to make money, not go swimming”. “If you want to make money then meet me at the beach at 4am tomorrow” the guru repeated. So, the young guy turns up at 4am, all suited up for business to receive his first lesson in business studies from the guru. The guru grabs his hand and says, “If you want to make money then follow me”, as he walks them into the sea waist deep. The young guy follows instantly realising the suit was a bad idea. Standing waist deep in the cold water, he’s thinking, this guy is crazy. I want to make money, and he’s got me swimming. “This is crazy,” says the young man. “What are we doing out here?” “You said you wanted to be successful, you said you wanted to make money, right? Then follow me”. The young guy follows the guru until his shoulders are beneath the water. “This is ridiculous,” the young guy states, “How do I make money? You’ve got me out here, I’m freezing and in my only suit in the middle of the ocean. I just want to learn how to be successful, not swim”. With that, the guru grabs the guy's head and holds him under the water. He keeps holding him down, keeping his head under the water, holding him down as he’s splashing about fighting the guru to get his head into the air. The guru holds him under until just before he passes out. Once the young man is starting to recover, the guru asks him a question. “When you were under the water, what was the one thing you wanted to do?”. “Breathe,” he replied, as he spluttered the salty water out of his month. Here’s lesson one, the guru preaches. “When you want to be successful as badly as you wanted to breathe in that moment, then you will be successful”.

This is a lesson for everything in life. I’m not materialistic or money-orientated, but I do thrive to be the best husband and father, the best provider and carer, the best coach and friend I can be. I want to give my family a nice home and security, and provide them with a few pleasures in life, and I hope I can pass something down to them when I'm gone. I want to be as lively, active, healthy and mobile for as long as I possibly can so I can have the energy to feel as much of this world as possible in my short years. I’m guessing this is exactly what you want too, but how badly do you want it? How badly do you want the love in your life to stay in your life? How badly do you want continued health and a nicely toned body? How badly do you want the promotion? How badly do you want that holiday of a lifetime, or the new house or the latest gadget? How badly do you want freedom, connectivity or comfort? Some people *wish* for these things to happen, some people *hope* these things will come their way, and some people, and these are the very few, *make* these dreams come true. Which person are you? How badly do you *really* want it? As bad as you want to breathe? Or do you just want it until it starts getting a little painful, and then head for the easier path? You know that path, it's the one everyone else is following! In order to make anything happen you have to want it, and most of the time, the real question is, what are you willing to sacrifice and how much pain are you willing to take, to get it?

2. Consistency is key, and patience is a virtue!

Little and often! It's the small things you do every day that make the difference!

Arnold Schwarzenegger once said:

"A well-built physique is more than vanity. It shows discipline, dignity and dedication. It requires patience, passion and self-respect. It cannot be bought, stolen or inherited, and it cannot be held onto without constant hard work".

This is as true about everything as it is about the body. You are never the finished product, and you will always have a lot more to learn.

Becoming a competent, caring, loving and disciplined father or mother is not something you are born knowing. It takes consistent learning every day. When it comes to this relationship you are as much a blank piece of paper as your child is. Both of you are learning a little bit more each day. Then, just when you think you've cracked it, the criteria changes and you have to re-learn how to do it all over again. Similarly, all the relationships in your life need constant fluidity and patience to make sure they survive the onslaught of life's stresses, and the continual emotional challenges that life joyfully places in front of you.

Building a career, a home, and financial security all require consistency and patience. The highest category for suicides is ages eighteen to twenty-five, and mostly men. This is the age bracket when everyone is full of expectation. They believe that they've done the hard work and life in all its fullness will be given to them. They have been told that once they've achieved their degree, or qualify in their selected skill, the world will be their oyster. But life isn't like that. It takes ten, twenty, sometimes thirty years to reach a level of mastery within your chosen field.

Regardless of what the Bible says, it takes more than six days to build a world around you. A warm, comfortable, welcoming home full of wonderful memories and financial stability isn't going to happen just because you've worked hard for a year or two. More realistically, it's going to take a couple of decades of slowly, but consistently lifting the hammer and chisel every day, and chipping away at the stone a little at a time before you start seeing the sculpture of your life materialise.

To repeat what Arnold said, your health, your wellness, your body and your mind need constant attention to make them work efficiently for as long as possible. You can't go down the gym solidly for four weeks and expect to be healthy, fit, mobile and strong for the other forty-eight weeks of the year. Just as you can't have a three-day shower at the beginning of the year and expect not to stink like a skunk by February. That hygiene stuff needs to be taken care of daily. Health and wellbeing, both physically and mentally, need consistent work; they need to be checked every day for chinks in the armour, and then given regular maintenance to keep them performing optimally. Patience is the key to success. Don't rush the process, enjoy the ride because it's going to be a long one. It might have taken twenty years to slowly increase your weight by a few stone, so it's going to need more than twenty days to remove it. So, as I said, practise enjoying the ride and not hope for a quick conclusion, because it never works, and you'll spend your life feeling disappointed; and who has time for that.

It's easy really, just be consistent with your actions and practise patience. Then you'll see that your dreams will become your realities.

3. Stand up and believe in yourself!

While we are here, we may as well quote another muscle-bound movie star. Sylvester Stallone, who famously lectures his son in a Rocky film when his son is moaning about how unfair life is. It's probably one of my favourite scenes from all the Rocky films and is written on a poster directly in front of my treadmill where I read it over and over again as I run the rubber off my trainers one step at a time.

"Let me tell you something you already know: The world ain't all sunshine and rainbows. It's a very mean and nasty place and I don't care how tough you are, it will beat you to your knees and keep you there permanently if you let it. You, me, or nobody is gonna hit as hard as life. But it ain't about how hard you hit. It's about how hard you can get hit and keep moving forward, how much you can take and keep moving forward. That's how winning is done! Now if you know what you're worth then go out and get what you're worth, but you need to be willing to take the hits, and stop pointing fingers and saying you ain't where you want to be because of him or her or anybody. Cowards do that and that ain't you, you're better than that!"

Life is going to beat you to your knees and will keep you there for as long as you let it. Standing back up time after time after time is *the* hardest thing you will ever do, and I do mean ever. Just when you think you have a grasp on things and have taken a few steps forward, life finds a way to make sure you know you're not in control. If you really want something, you have to earn it; you have to prove time after time how important it is to you and not let anyone take that drive and ambition and passion away from you. People will hold you down, disrespect you and try to take your dreams away, because they don't have a dream of their own, and because it makes them insecure.

Never stop believing in yourself, your dreams or your capabilities. It doesn't matter how many times you get knocked over by life, by people, by finances or just by bad luck. If you truly believe in what you are fighting for then never waver, never sway and never settle for less. When you get knocked down, roll onto your back and look at the heavens; remember your resolve, learn the necessary lesson that's just been given to you and get back to your feet.

Sylvester Stallone wrote Rocky in the 70's and was so adamant he wanted to play the character of Rocky Balboa that he continually refused to sell the script to the filmmakers. Regardless of the money they offered, he believed in himself and stood tall and strong, even when they said he was too ugly and couldn't talk properly. Months and months went by as he became so financially desperate that he had to sell his dog outside a 7-eleven for $40 to get some food. But eventually, after nearly being forced to sleep on the streets, a film producer took the gamble on him at a fraction of the sale price he could have sold the script for if he wasn't to play the role of Rocky himself. Sylvester knew who he was, what he wanted and what needed to happen for him to achieve it. This single-mindedness gave him the strength to get back to his feet time after time. There were no if's or but's. There was no sobbing or moaning, and there were no regrets. We all know how that perseverance worked out for him in the end.

Oh, and by the way, the first thing he did when he got that much-smaller payment from the film maker, was buy back his dog for a hell of a lot more than he sold it for. The dog's name was Brutus and is the actual dog in the original Rocky film. The guy he sold it to and bought it back from also has a cameo in the movie as part of the sale agreement when Stallone repurchased his best friend from him. He is the guy sitting at the bar in the pub on his own.

Until you start believing in yourself, standing back up and fighting for what you want, you won't have a life, you'll just exist.

4. Be a daydreamer!

I'm not a poet, I know nothing about poetry, and I have never read poetry, but somehow these words found their way into my head. I don't know when or how, but it's there and I know it inside out. It's written by an author called Thomas Edward Lawrence who wrote a few books, one being quite famous called Seven Pillars of Wisdom. I believe this is where these words were written. He wasn't really classed as a poet, although most better-educated people than me would say his writing had a poetic edge. I certainly class this as more of a poem than a quote. T. E. Lawrence was also an archaeologist and a British soldier in the first World War, more famously known for his nickname of Lawrence of Arabia. He was a key figure in the Arab Revolt during the First World War, fighting alongside Arab guerrilla forces in the Middle East. These words resonated with me the first time I heard them, so much so that I have a few of them tattooed on my chest. The bold script below is the section I have tattooed:

'All men dream: but not equally. Those who dream by night in the dusty recesses of their minds wake in the day to find that it was vanity: but ***the dreamers of the day are dangerous men, for they may act out their dream with open eyes, to make it possible.'***

I believe I am a daydreamer, and I truly believe I am dangerous. I'm dangerous to myself, I'm dangerous to the environment around me and I'm dangerous to the people in it. The question is, is this a bad thing? I personally don't consider it to be.

Daydreamers are the people that make shit happen; the inventors, the explorers, the free thinkers, the people who push boundaries, look for limits of their own capabilities and ask the question, why? Why is it this way? Why do I have to continue along this route? Why should this be the limit? Why can't I change it? And what happens if I do? They refuse to accept the reality they live in as the only option, continually searching for change and treading on new ground, exploring further than their comfort zones, and relishing the opportunity to grow their conscience, their character, their thresholds and their world. To put it more simply, everyone is creative in some capacity, but those who are dreamers of the day are the ones who see the outcome of their creativity, the ones who actively set out a plan to achieve their goals. These individuals have incredible potential for changing the world around them, and that's why Thomas Edward Lawrence calls them dangerous.

Be a daydreamer. Act on your dreams. Don't settle for mundanity. Don't settle for what's already written for you. Rewrite the script, ask questions, continue searching, and piss off a few people along the way. *Be dangerous!*

5. Don't fear the Reaper!

My biggest fear is death. I think about it most days, but not mine, my wife's. I fear the day I might be left alone, and I do believe I could be the one left alone. I am 7 years younger than Teri and my genetic tree is slightly stronger than hers.

I take after my grandad on my mother's side. My build, strength and personality come from my sturdy Scottish heritage. My grandad was one of four brothers who unintentionally created an ongoing joke around the people they were closest to about not bloody dying. No matter what life threw at them, they wouldn't die. That could be misinterpreted as being extremely heartless and horrible, and was by no means wishful thinking, but it was true. Their stubbornness to fight on and refusal to accept death was a running joke. Jonny, my grandad, lived until his mid 80's, which doesn't sound anything out of the ordinary, but if you look at how he lived his life, he beat the odds. He smoked for seventy-two years and drank whisky every day for most of that as well. He spent twenty-five years in the navy and twenty-five years in the coal pits, grafting hard every day of his life. Life treated him hard, constantly trying to get him to yield, but his dog-headed Scottish blood just chewed it up and used it as fuel. In the end It was COPD that got him, but he did put up a hell of a fight and lived twice as long as the doctors predicted. One of the last memories I have of him was watching as he inhaled a lung full of smoke from the cigarette in his left hand, and then immediately after exhaling the dense cloud, he would suck for dear life on the mouthpiece of an oxygen tank with his right hand so he could try and breathe again. Bloody dangerous, but health and safety was never part of the dictionary for my grandad.

This was par for the course for the rest of the siblings. Archie, his youngest brother, has only recently passed after making it into his nineties. I believe he smoked most of his life and finished more than a few bottles of Scottish malt whisky in his time. In his younger years, Archie was very much into his motorbikes, and these were the days when no helmets were necessary. I remember a story about him riding along one day when the car in front of him did an emergency stop. Archie hit the back of the car, which sent him catapulting into the air and over the roof, eventually coming to a stop as his head broke through the back window of the car in front. He spent a long time in hospital and was left with a hole in his head where the doctors needed to release the pressure on his brain. His party trick was to grab your finger and insert it into the hole beneath the skin in his forehead where the cranium had been drilled. That's something that freaks you out as a young boy. A couple of weeks after leaving the hospital he was back on the motorbike, flying around without a care in the world, and once again without a helmet on. No surprise, he found himself back in hospital after wrapping himself around a tree, but this time needing spinal surgery. After a few weeks of bed rest and with a fused spine he was back out, being an idiot and enjoying life for what it was. I still think his old Bonneville, which he tried to sit on every now and then, is still in the garage.

One thing I remember my grandad saying to me was, “Son, you’ll live a long time, but you’ll live in pain. Do what you can do for as long as you can do it, and don’t let anyone get in your way”. Hopefully, as I’m looking after myself a little better than he did, I’ll get to do it a bit longer and in a little less pain than he carried with him.

Teri has a lot of genetic influence from her father. He was also one of many siblings, most of them struggling to see seventy years old. None of them really took care of themselves very well, as they indulged in smoking and drinking, while existing on low exercise and high stress. Obviously, this largely contributed to their shortened lives, but their genetic strength wasn't the best when it came to bouncing back from health issues. I understand life was a lot harder in many ways for that generation, so this is by no means a finger-pointing exercise. I guess the small joys of a social drink or a five-minute break to have a cigarette counted for a hell of a lot to their happiness. Teri, though, has woken up to the dangers of the wrong lifestyle choices. Her health, fitness and wellbeing has vastly improved over the past decade or so, and I believe she has fought very hard to give herself a better life outcome, that could have otherwise been the case.

It scares the shit out of me to think I might be left on my own. Every day I live with the fear that life will stop when that day happens and I won't feel anything the day after that, or the day after that, or the day after that. There will be no more sunrises or sunsets, no wind or rain, or summers and winters. I feel time will just stop. There'll be no more colour and there'll be no birds tweeting. Food will lose its flavour, and flowers will lose their scent. I fear life will just freeze on that day, and this day haunts me, every day.

Recently I heard something that gave me hope; hope that I could maybe find a way of continuing afterwards. I can't remember where I heard it, but I remember feeling there was a possibility that I could find a desire to move on, a reason to continue.

When you love someone, you trade a part of their soul with yours. They take some of yours and you take some of theirs, so when they die a piece of you dies with them, which is why it hurts so much. But, on the other side of the coin, you still carry a piece of them with you. A piece of them is still alive within you, so they can still experience life, and the world, through your eyes and ears. They can still taste and smell, and they can still feel, experience and grow through you as you continue on your journey. So, you need to switch on the colour and open your ears to the sounds of nature and music, and you need to enjoy the flavoursome foods and smell the roses, because It's the only way your loved one can continue enjoying the world. You need to live so they can keep living through you.

I still fear the reaper, but now I don't let the reaper lay heavy on my day. You can't live a single day, productively, if the fear of death is casting a shadow over it. As we progress through the ages of life our fear of death becomes stronger, and sometimes so overpowering we stop taking chances, we stop living on the edge, and we very rarely experience life outside our comfort zones. Yet we tell everyone around us that this is where life exists. We become so reclusive in our ways through the fear of change that it stops us living. We fear the change could in some way encourage the inevitable future to arrive too quickly, Better to be safe, and all that! We don't smell the flowers or see the colour in them, we don't sample new tastes or truly listen to the world around us, we don't dance in the rain or jump off the metaphoric cliff anymore. Without taking chances, feeling uncomfortable, pushing boundaries and feeling high from life, a piece of us has already died before we are dead. Never stop taking chances and rolling the dice. Spend as much time with your people as you can, and not in the pursuit of the illusionary safety we try to build around us. Don't be controlled by the fear of loss but be driven by the excitement of opportunity, and most importantly, don't fear the reaper. He's coming whatever happens, so you may as well throw yourself in at the deep end.

6. Make your bed in the morning!

Right, I don't know about you, but I need something a little lighter after the previous lesson. Making your bed in the morning.

Making your bed in the morning has so many benefits, such as stimulating positive habits for the day, and installing self-discipline and goal setting. It can help you feel a sense of accomplishment as it boosts your self-esteem, helping you create a sense of order and control. This can influence your emotional wellbeing, creating a more inviting environment to return to at the end of the day. It promotes cleanliness and hygiene and will set a positive example to others.

In my opinion, and above all else, the most important reason to make your bed in the morning is to show character. It's something you do not necessarily have to do but do it anyway. It's something you can own for the day straight from the get-go. Other examples of this would be putting the supermarket trolley away after you've finished with it. Discarding your tea bag in the bin and not in the sink. Treating everyone equally regardless of wealth, position, gender, age, or anything else. Giving an unnecessary compliment to a stranger or instantly cleaning as you go instead of leaving it for another time or for another person. Putting the toilet seat down, holding doors, smiling, showing gratitude and respect even when nothing is shown in return.

These and many other behaviours will show a person's character, and character is what people see, regardless of wealth or stature, designer clothes or manicured nails. It won't matter what car you drive or even if you drive at all; it won't matter what house you have or if you are homeless; it won't matter what position you hold in the company or the group of friends you associate with, the holidays you take, the dog you walk, the area you are from, your gender, religion, age or colour. People will always see your character. A visual perception of someone is short lived, but their character will leave a lasting impression. It can make the most beautiful person ugly, and the less genetically gifted person glow. As human beings we are subconsciously equipped to see the tell-tale signs of nice and horrible people. This is a pure survival skill built over millennia to create safe environments for our loved ones. We have an acute sense of people's characters. We feel energies from individuals within seconds of meeting them and instantly feel comfortable or uneasy around them.

If you want a happy, friendly, productive and successful existence, then practise showing good character traits. You will always receive what you give. The universe will always confront you with the people who have the same traits you show. Rude people will attract rude people, aggressive people will attract aggressive people, just as kind, polite, honest, grateful, forgiving, tolerant, fair, responsible and cooperative people will attract their equals. You get what you deserve. Give out what you would like to receive, regardless of how you get treated - that's good character.

Start practising these positive habits and traits by just making your bed in the morning.

7. Look after the pennies… or the minutes!

My grandma, along with, I'm guessing, everyone else's grandma used to say, "Look after the pennies and the pounds will look after themselves". Pretty self-explanatory really. As long as you are careful and make conscious decisions before spending any of your hard-earned pennies, the pounds will naturally look after themselves. Don't be frivolous with your money, don't spend it on shit just because. Be wise and get the biggest bang for your buck.

I have also come up with my own saying recently. Earn a little, send a little. Always send a little bit of money to your future self-first. I guarantee there'll be days when your future self needs those pennies a lot more than your current self does. I promise you'll thank yourself in the future. I know there'll be times of struggle, and times when you'll be panicking to put food on the table. These are the times for which you've sent the donation forward. Help yourself out of the shit before the shit shows up.

In the end though, it's just money. It comes and goes. It can give you some fun times and buy you some nice stuff and experiences, but over all it's a little fucker. It makes you chase it all your life and never allows you to believe you have enough. In some way It dictates every decision you make, from the holidays you have, the house, car or furniture you buy, even the shops you buy food from and the size of coffee you buy at the cafe. Everything from how you raise your kids to where you'll work and at what age you can retire. It even shows in the coffin you'll be buried in, and I bloody hate it. The dark side of money will always outweigh the pleasure you can get from it. It rules and ruins the world, and we can't live without it. The beauty of it though, is that it doesn't matter how useless you are with it, you can always earn some more.

There is a currency you can't earn more of though, and that's time. Time flows in one direction only - forward. Every day, hour, minute or second is time spent with no chance of earning any more. You have been given a bank account of seconds that gets spent without your control, and most of the time, without even consciously even thinking about it. When your account is empty, that's it, your time stops. There is no overdraft or savings account and no loan sharks to fall back on. You have your balance at the beginning and that's it. It doesn't matter if you're staring at the walls, bungee jumping off a bridge, driving to work, collecting some groceries, having a nice romantic evening and getting lucky with your partner, or slaving away in some shitty job making someone else's seconds more pleasurable; you are, without exception, spending your account.

I saw a clever movie recently starring Justin Timberlake called 'In Time'. The concept of the movie was that once you turn twenty-five years old you are given one more year of time before you die, which is shown as a digital countdown implanted in your forearm. When the time runs out, you die. You can earn more time by going to work, or people can give you some of their time on birthdays or just a gift to help you live longer, but the clock keeps ticking. On the flip side though, everything you purchase costs you time off your life expectancy as your countdown reduces by the purchase price. For example, coffee could cost you two minutes of life, a meal out might mean you are thirty minutes closer to your death; a car maybe two years, your mortgage each month might be a couple of days closer to lights out, etc.

If this was the case, how would you spend your money, or your time, as it were? Would it be different to how you are wasting money, or wasting your time now? How many of your precious seconds and minutes would you spend looking at your phone? With a countdown constantly ticking away on your arm showing how much time you have left until you die, would you spend time worrying about someone else's opinion of you, or caring about things that are beyond your influence? How much of that remaining time would you spend depressed about stuff in your past that you can't change, or anxious about stuff in the future you can't anticipate? How much time would you waste worrying about time?

Every day is precious, and every minute is a gift that sadly some people no longer have, and unfortunately, but inevitably, neither will you soon. Spend your minutes wisely. Go to bed every night knowing today was worth living. As you pull up the duvet at the end of the day, I want you to feel the contentment and the satisfaction that you didn't just naively let the day pass. Get in the habit of being consciously aware of the day happening around you and make decisions to show the day was worth living. Most of the people in the world wake complacently the next day without feeling the gift they have been given and selfishly go through it as if they are simply entitled to it. They don't respect it, honour it or feel privileged by it, and they definitely don't share the wealth of it with anyone else. To show some gratitude for waking up, and the acknowledgement that today didn't necessarily need to happen for you, you should fill the day with as much as possible. Spend some time on the necessities, some time on creating joy and memories, some time on yourself, and some of it shared with others. Then, just before you close your eyes each night, think about how comfortable you feel. How spoiled you are to have a cosy bed, surrounded by the protection of your warm home, with food in your belly and a flushable toilet to use in the middle of the night. Also be aware of the peaceful surroundings you live in that have been built on so many generations of sacrifices that have been made before you. You owe it to yourself, and to past generations, to respect the day by dutifully giving something to it, therefore making sure you don't squander the gift. As you gratefully reminisce on the day's activities, visualise three boxes, then honestly tick each one in turn if you can say you achieved the task set by each box.

Box one: this can only be ticked if you can say you did something for yourself today. Just you? Something that made you feel warm, excited, rested, uplifted or happy. Basically, did you give yourself some of your very own day? Did you learn something new, spend time on a hobby, take a long bath while reading a book, go for a nice country walk, bake a cake, play a game with some mates? Anything that made you feel good about the day. If you did, tick that box.

Box two: did you do anything to help someone else, or make someone else have a better day? Something that you didn't have to do, something that for no reason whatsoever made someone else have a better day. Maybe you helped someone across the road or carried someone's shopping to their car. You could have complimented someone's hair as you saw them exiting the hairdressers or praised someone's gardening efforts when witnessing them knee deep in their flowery borders. Share the love and don't be selfish with your gift of this day. No love given, means no tick in the box.

Box three: did you do anything to help the future, both yours, and everyone else's? What did you do today to make your future healthier, happier and better equipped? Did you exercise, meditate, prepare and consume nutritious food, save some money, work towards a promotion or even just declutter your house or life? If so, then that's half the box ticked. The other half is ticked by answering a more important question. Did you do anything today to make a better future for the world? For example, did you keep on top of recycling, save energy, give time or money to a charity, cycle or walk to work reducing pollution or scatter some wildflower seeds. Anything to show appreciation to the world for its continued support.

Every day should be honoured and respected, and every day you should show how grateful you are to be in it. Ticking these boxes won't take long, and before you know it, it will quickly become an unconscious habit. I guarantee this process will make you feel amazing about yourself and will stop you becoming wrapped up in the mundanities of life.

8. Sleep quicker!

This is another famous quote from Arnie.

After I have spoken about the three boxes to my clients or friends, this is usually the next conversation we need to have. When I'm giving them another daily task to do, the response I get from most people, regarding the three boxes, and taking five minutes in the evening to think about the boxes is, 'I'm too busy for that stuff', or 'I haven't got time', or 'When am I supposed to think about that?' 'I've got kids, a job, a house to look after, walk the dogs, ageing parents; when am I supposed to fit in a bit of exercise or cook a nutritious meal, or relax in the tub or read a book, or take five minutes to think? You don't know my life, it's crazy; I never stop. I'd love to have some time for myself, but that's for other people'.

Whilst acknowledging and respecting how much they have to juggle throughout the day, my first question is, how much time do they spend on their phones? "Around an hour a day, I suppose," is usually the answer. But once my investigative skills are put in use, we find it's closer to twenty or twenty-five hours a week. I have seen one phone that was used, on average, eighty hours a week. "This is how I relax," is more often than not the feedback from this scary discovery. "But what about the boxset of 'Yellowstone' you destroyed over the weekend?" is my reply. "Wasn't that your downtime?" Sorry if I'm being a little sharp, but this sort of conversation is more common than you think.

I class myself as being very efficient with my time, and I love 'Yellowstone', but I have no idea how you can get through a whole series in two days. It takes me three hours a day just to look after myself, without considering working, sleeping, dog walking, shopping, cleaning the house, etc. I feel lucky if I can watch two episodes of something at the weekend. When I say three hours a day to look after myself, I'm referring to the things I need to do to remain mentally and physically strong. Hygiene, exercise, guitar, writing, meditating, playing on my motorbike. If I don't give myself this time, I'm no good to anybody. This is way more important and productive than spending 'relaxing' time on a phone.

Think of your twenty-four-hour day as your monthly financial budget. If you were hitting the red at the end of each month, you'd look at where you could save spending. You'd contact the power supply companies to look for a better deal, or downgrade the Sky TV, or slow down on a couple of nights out during the month and have a few less takeaways. Then you could reassess your finances to allow you to afford that summer holiday, or the finance on the new car you've been dreaming of. You would work hard and make changes in your life to achieve the things you've been dreaming of.

Look at your day the same way. What could be changed? If you spend ten hours at work, eight hours in bed, two hours on the phone and two hours watching TV you would only have two hours to do the rest; the school runs, the dog walks, hygiene, food, shopping, exercise, cleaning up and relaxing. Looks like a very busy day, but how much of that is wasted, how much of it could be multi-tasked? Turning a chore into chill-out time would make life a lot more enjoyable and less stressful. Walking the dog whilst listening to a book, relaxing in a bath rather than rushing a shower, smashing some music out whilst cleaning up, learning how to cook new dishes.

Take time to sit back and practise your budgeting skills in order to make your day more efficient. Procrastination is the vampire of your day; it sucks the life out of it, leaving it flat, pale and lifeless.

Take a look at your day and be honest. Ten hours of work can't be changed; eight hours of sleep, 'sleep quicker', six hours of quality sleep is perfect. The key word here is quality. Go to sleep on purpose, not just because your eyes have given up. Two hours on the phone and two hours of TV; pick one and save two hours. That leaves you six hours of day left, not two. You've already gained an extra four hours. Six whole hours left each day to do all the other stuff. Do you know how much damage I could do in six hours? That's a workday! Give me a day off work and I could do something really nuts, like, mmmm, write a book.

Budget your day, know how the day is going to look before you go to sleep the night before. Write a time plan and tick the jobs off when accomplished. Challenge yourself to get ahead of the schedule so you can give yourself a little more time in the tub or in the gym. We all have duties and responsibilities; at least make '*you*' one of your responsibilities.

9. **Keep your shit to yourself and leave it at the door.**

Whether it's good shit or bad shit, it's still just your shit. I've learnt, as I'm sure many others have too, that when good things are happening to you, when your world is rolling along nicely and going as expected, the worst thing you can do is to share it with others. You'll find there'll always be those people that can't handle your success or feel threatened by your dreams. They'll hold you back, bring you down, tell you how much of a bad idea that is and how it'll never work. Unfortunately, and sadly, they have no passion or dreams left of their own. Life has most probably kicked them too many times, leaving them tired and frustrated. Tired of fighting, tired of waking up every day already inside a storm; or maybe they've never had anyone close to teach them how to rise up when they've fallen, nobody to nurse them back to full strength so they can once again dream and be enthusiastic. I'm guessing that this is why they react by trying to suppress your fire and belittle your successes, just like any other ex-addict would when sitting next to an addict, only your addiction is life. There is a reason for keeping your wishes to yourself when blowing the candles out. They are more likely to come true if the nay-sayers aren't around to change your energy. I gave up on pursuing some of my own dreams in the past because the people closest to me at the time persuaded me they were too irrational and crazy, and I should stop dreaming. "You've got your whole life ahead of you, be content with what you have and feel lucky you are where you are", they would say. Maybe they were right in most cases, but isn't life a gamble? We have no idea what is going to happen, how it's going to happen or when it's going to happen. When shit is going your way and the sun is shining, soak it up, feel the heat, and enjoy the sand between your toes. But don't try to bring everyone to the beach with you, because someone will always try to piss on your sandcastle.

Equally, when you've had a bad day, things aren't going your way and your energy is pretty dark, don't cloud over someone else's sunshine. This is your storm; weather it. Find a way through and learn how to rise above the clouds to see the light. Talk about it by all means. Find a loved-one or someone you trust to share the load, but remember, they don't deserve your darkness. Dealing with your own shit and pushing through is a muscle that can and will grow. Every time you've found a way to fly above the clouds, the easier it will be 'next time' to spread your wings and lift yourself off the ground. I feel this transformation most days in my studio. It's a safe place for people to come and learn how to grow their wings. Their energy changes throughout the session as exercise replaces the stress hormones with happy hormones, giving a different perspective to their troubles. People can come through the door in quite a dark mood, visibly carrying a weight on their shoulders and tension in their stature, and it becomes very quickly apparent that they need to share the doom and pull me into their storm; it's hard sometimes. When the day has finished and I've used exercise to change how my clients react to their problems, given them an ear to share the burden, and hopefully a little advice to part their clouds, I can be left in my own darkness a little bit. I don't want to carry this from my clients to my family and ruin their day, so I exercise every day. It's the habit that keeps me from crying into my vegetables, unless I'm chopping onions, or bouncing off the walls, or making irrational decisions to create arguments, just to blow off some steam. Exercise, for me, blows the clouds away so I can have a sensible and logical chat in the warmth of the sun with my loved one or a trusted friend. Like I said, everyone needs to talk and should definitely open up more often, but no-one should be forced to sit in your storm. Find something that helps you part the clouds; paint, read, play an instrument, walk in nature, meditate, light some candles, take a bath, bake or do some gardening. Anything that can help *you* arrive home, *you*, and not the physical mass that is the consequence of the day's shit. I would like to think that you have someone who has spent all day looking forward to your return, so they can share the remainder of their day with you. But, if they don't want to, could it be that you've spent too much time in the past forcing your weather on them, and not releasing your darkness in more productive ways, before calmly chatting about your problems. The type of relationship you have with everyone around you is an equal reaction to how you treat them. Sort yourself out first before giving it to someone else.

10. Passion.

Passion is the most important thing in life to me. I have already written this in 'Don't Fail at Failure', as well as in this book in the previous chapter, but feel I need to repeat myself here because this really is where the magic happens, where life begins and where it ends. This is what changes you from a caterpillar to a butterfly, and this is the difference between having an existence *or* living a life. *Passion* is the key that makes you use words like laughter, enjoyment, excitement, devotion, gratitude, joy and love. Money, commercialism and materialism cannot complete you, only passion can: passion in your relationships, passion in your vocation, passion for nature, passion for the human spirit, and passion for self-fulfilment. This is life.

Everyone has passion. Some people's passion has been drowned out by the unachievable expectations placed onto their shoulders by the system. Some people's passion is scared to raise its head above the smothering cloud of normality because of what others might say. But the lucky few live with their passion on their sleeve for all to see, and they live an exciting, spontaneous, plentiful and joyful life. This is because every day has purpose for them, and every achievement further fuels the passion inside. Sadly, these lucky ones are few and far between, but they stand out like a sore thumb.

As you can see, I am deeply passionate about passion, which is why I now spend my time pursuing my dreams and leading by example in the hope that my daughters will be educated by it and driven to follow theirs. I believe that, when it comes to becoming a successful human and being successful in life, knowing yourself and being confident in who you are, what you like, what you dislike and what you are passionate about, is crucial. You can work as hard as you can to build a respectable C.V. full of qualifications, work experience, and interesting hobbies, but if you don't have passion for what you have and what you're doing, it will niggle at your subconscious, eventually eating you up from the inside out. All those childhood dreams you once had that were full of excitement, knowing you had the world at your feet and a lifetime to experience it, have dwindled away into a ghostly shadow. A shadow that floats around its entire life dominating an unfulfilling career, earning as much money as possible to buy as much stuff as it can to try to fill the emptiness that's left behind when passion has left the building. This is not what I want for my cherubs, my two angels, so, as always, I educate by example. I want to show them how powerful passion can be; how much it can shape life and attract people. Regardless of where your passion takes you, if you show it, people will follow. Why? Because it's now in very short supply, and others will be attracted to you and long to be part of your life because you have it.

11. Dance in the rain.

You will always have problems. You will always have some sort of conflict going on in your life. You must learn to enjoy life while still solving them. There is beauty in everything we experience; you just need to adjust your perception. You can either cry in the storm or dance in the rain.

I have spent my entire life fighting against one battle or another. Parents splitting up, being the new kid on the block and being introduced into a new family, being bullied, running away from home, not finishing school, having to become a grown up before my time, getting a divorce, becoming bankrupt, dealing with alcohol, drugs, gambling and other addictions, caring for a disabled wife, standing in a hospital room with a child hours away from possibly dying, massive debt, losing a business, being unemployed, being labelled as the black sheep in the family and disowned. These are just the things off the top of my head as I'm sitting here typing away. This doesn't include the usual stresses, heartaches, disappointments and punches you feel and take travelling through a normal lifetime, such as moving house, suffering illnesses, feeling the loss of a pet, not getting the promotion or the dream job, arguing with friends, receiving a £4,000 repair bill on your house or your car that you can't afford; children growing up and flying the nest, feeling all the trials and tribulations of the weathered mind and body as age starts affecting you. These, along with an endless list of other kicks, punches and slaps we feel as we write the pages of our story, are the experiences that make us feel isolated, alone and singled out. We repeatedly stare at the heavens questioning, “Why me?”. What have I done wrong? Why do I keep getting picked on?

When will I ever get a break? The truth is, you're not being victimised or segregated. Everyone is feeling the burn. Everyone you walk past in the supermarket, everyone driving past in their cars in the other direction on the motorway, everyone standing in the huge stadium with you as you watch your favourite team, everyone dancing alongside you in the club, and everyone you see splashed all over the pages of social media, on cinema screens, and singing your favourite song in your earphones, is fighting. Fighting a world you cannot see. They are no different from you or anyone else. Everyone wakes up every morning, and within seconds finds themselves in a conflict, something unresolved, something standing in their way, a barrier separating them from their current life and their perceived happier life.

If I'm honest, and you know I am from how much I share in my stories, all of the above is just dust. It's just ships passing in the night, blips on the landscape and potholes in the road. The biggest conflict, the most pain, the unrelenting battle that haunts every single one of us, is ourselves. The fight with ourselves. It's the constant bombardment, the continued stabbing, poking and prodding, the monotony of the persistent drip of water on the forehead trying to drive you insane. Our own minds are our biggest enemy. It's our most poisonous critic, our greatest adversary and our ultimate challenger. It never wavers, it never takes a break, it always has something to say about everything and it constantly tries to hold you in a state of conflict. This is the storm that never yields. This, above all else, is the battle that will dictate your experience of this life, on this planet.

The secret though, is that you cannot beat it because there isn't really a conflict. There is no winner because there is no competition. There will never, ever be a moment when you can say, 'That's that shit sorted, I'm in control now, I've nailed it'. There will never be a victorious feeling of winning this struggle because '*you*' are always there, and it's 'you' trying to beat 'you'. If you win you still lose. The sooner you accept that it just is, it's just life, the sooner you can start practising the art of dancing in the rain. You'll find the roller coaster so much more enjoyable when you understand it's going to happen anyway. The wheels are moving and cannot be stopped until you've had your ride, so stick your hands in the air, scream as loud as you can and feel the rush of unpredictability.

See the beauty in everything, feel the lessons, grab the opportunities, enjoy every one-to-one, and relish every emotion because it shows you that you are still alive and still have another opportunity to grow.

12. One breath, one step, one second at a time!

As mentioned before, there is no other way. As long as you look at, deal with and accept life in this manner, you can deal with anything, absolutely anything. Take a breath, step forward and see what happens next.

So, there it is! Fifty-one years of me. Many lifetimes squeezed into what feels like a blink of an eye. Hopefully, I have plenty of years left to learn new lessons, and maybe I'll get the opportunity to pass those on as well. But here it is so far:

- If you want to be successful, you really need to want it.
- Be consistent and patient. This is how you get what you want.
- Know and believe in yourself.
- Never stop dreaming.
- Don't fear death, it'll stop you living.
- Start the day as you mean to finish it, in control.
- Your time is precious to you. Don't waste a minute of it.
- Make time for yourself, even if you have to sleep quicker
- Keep your shit to yourself
- Passion, passion and more passion. Otherwise, what else is there?
- Never stop dancing, regardless of what's thrown at you.
- Just take it 'One Breath, One Step and One Second at a time'.

After thoughts

Reading my book in the middle of February as the finished article the day before I'm about to send it to be published, I felt I wanted to add a couple of thoughts.

Firstly, referring back to the introduction, and the point of not wanting to dilute the quality of the first book. I honestly believe I have done the first book justice. I am very proud of the words I have written here and feel I have once again been as honest and open as I can. Also, it wasn't hard to get the flow back. Once the first few hundred words had started making sentences, I was off! The therapy started almost immediately and once again writing allowed me to dive into myself again, creating a voyage of self-discovery. I would advise anyone who is struggling to just write shit down, even if it's just for you and you throw it away afterwards. Even if it's just about a load of bollocks and nothing of any importance or structure, or even if it has nothing to do with how you are feeling. Just write.

Secondly, since writing this book I have been seeing a therapist to help me get past my addictive nature, and to try to reduce the roller coaster of emotions I go through monthly, weekly and sometimes daily. I really do suffer from big highs and self-destructing lows, it's tiring for me and for my family. It turns out that I suffer from a degree of autism and ADHD, which looking back at my two books explains quite a bit. A lot of what I talk about makes sense now. Apparently, these traits are what gives me the drive and ability to push harder than most, and question everything. They give me the capability to be hyper-vigilant and hyper-productive. In a lot of ways, they are a gift. They will allow me to achieve a hell of a lot more during my life because, even on an average day, I get to do twice as much as I would without them. The downside though, is the downside; the lows, they are such a burden, so dark and without the strength to fight them, would end me and anyone close to me. This is why I hide in stuff. Strangely, now that I understand I'm not broken, I actually just think differently and process differently, it has released me, and the lows don't last as long as they used to. I accept them for what they are and progress them more productively. I'm only sharing this in case someone feels the same about themselves, and they question whether talking to someone is the right thing to do. You're not broken, you just need to learn what your rules are, in your game, so you can play fairly and constructively.

Lastly, I would like to once again thank a few people for putting up with me, supporting me and helping me with this second book.

My wife, Teri. Such an amazing person. There is not another soul on this planet that deserves more than I give. I do try my hardest to give her what she provides for me, but I always think I'm coming up short. I want to thank you for holding me up when I am down and encouraging me when I am flying. We have, hopefully decades left. I can't wait to see what trouble we can get up to!

My two amazing daughters, who are now both fully grown up and showing their wings. I am now learning how to live from them; they are showing me how to live a better life than I thought was available to me. My vision of what is possible in the time I have left is expanding every time I lift my head, because of them. They are my strength, my guides and my youth.

I want to give a big hug to all the friends who listen to me, help me and continually ask if I am ok without looking for anything in return. Sometimes I do feel I neglect you sometimes, but you never pull me up on it; you just keep checking in, regardless. I am very grateful and honoured, so thank you.

My very talented mother-in-law who edited this book for me; and has made me look a lot more of a talented writer than I actually am. Thank you again V.

Also, Erica for asking a very thought-provoking question after she went through the book to let me know how it felt. She said, you talk about passion a lot, but what is your passion? What are you passionate about? The answer is, all I know is that I am passionate about the pursuit of passion. I do need to find mine.

Maybe I have another book in me, yet!